THE ME

AMAT

THEATRE

HANDBOOK

I0580923

THE METHUEN DRAMA

AMATEUR THEATRE HANDBOOK

KEITH ARROWSMITH

Methuen Drama

Methuen Drama

Published by Methuen Drama 2001

1 3 5 7 9 10 8 6 4 2

This edition published in Great Britain in 2001 by
Methuen Drama, an imprint of
Bloomsbury Publishing Plc

Methuen Drama
Bloomsbury Publishing Plc
36 Soho Square
London, W1D 3QY

www.methuendrama.com

Methuen Publishing Limited Reg. No. 3543167

A CIP catalogue record for this book
is available from the British Library

ISBN 978 0 413 75570 4

Typeset in Bembo by MATS, Southend-on-Sea, Essex

Printed and bound in Great Britain by
CPI Antony Rowe, Chippenham and Eastbourne

Contents

2 THE SHOW

Acknowledgements

Many people and organisations have helped in the production of this handbook. They include family and friends (especially Bill Lawson), umbrella organisations (in particular NODA), societies (notably Sheffield Teachers Operatic Society's Judy McMurray, Wendy of Beck Youth Theatre and Keith Derbyshire of the Lantern Theatre), other professionals (including Nick Winsbrow of NODA Insurance) and work colleagues (especially Rachel, Josie, Colleen and Keren). Dick Greener's comments on early drafts were gratefully received. Without those people, the project would have been much more difficult. However, without Mark Cobb, the project would have been impossible. My thanks go to them all, and I hope that the handbook meets with their approval. Any errors remain my responsibility.

Maurice W. Maxwell, whose family founded Sweet & Maxwell the law publishers, by his will established a charitable trust to be known as the Alexander Maxwell Law Scholarship Trust in memory of both his great-great-grandfather and great-grandfather. The Trust is committed to promoting legal research and writing at various levels via the provision of financial assistance to authors whether they be experienced legal practitioners, or those in the early years of practice. The author of this work received financial assistance from the Trust to enable him to complete this work. The Trust calls for applications for awards each year, with a closing date of 31 August for awards to be made early in the following January. Anyone interested in its work should write to:

The Clerk to the Trustees
Alexander Maxwell Law Scholarship Trust
c/o Sweet & Maxwell
100 Avenue Road
London NW3 3PF
or visit the Trust's web site at: www.amlst.org.uk

Contributors

I am indebted to the following people who supplied contributions for this handbook. Some appear as specific sections, to which I have added relevant details. Others I have used as a starting point for my own research and writings:

Richard Findlay (Scottish Law) is the entertainment and media law partner of T2M, part of law firm Tods Murray with offices in Edinburgh and Glasgow. He provides legal advice to theatres, dance and ballet companies, as well as agents, actors, designers, directors and playwrights. Richard lectures extensively, is a committee member of BAFTA (Scotland) and a director of the Royal Lyceum Theatre Company.

Stuart Hawkes and Roger Hill (Youth Groups). Stuart is the Director of the National Association of Youth Theatres. Ten years of professional involvement has seen him work in a variety of settings with a wide range of young people from across the UK. His work has been primarily with young people who, if not for public funding, would have little access to the arts. Stuart's work has featured on both television and radio and most recently he co-wrote/devised a short piece for presentation at the Labour Party Conference (2000). Roger co-founded and is President of NAYT.

Tony Jaggers and **Alicia Petty (Open-Air Performances).** Tony has been Derby Shakespeare Theatre Company's business manager for the last twenty-five years and has been responsible for the overall planning and control of all its outdoor productions, including acting as tour manager to the Minack Theatre, Cornwall. The company has won a number of prestigious awards over the years and continues to bring Shakespeare to an ever widening audience. Alicia is an experienced actor, producer and writer.

Peter Lathan (Performing in Schools) is head of drama at a north-east comprehensive school. Since his first school production in 1967, he has directed over fifty shows, from straight plays to musicals. He has run courses for teachers, is the author of the web site, 'The School Show Page', and writes the *Guide to British Theatre* for New York-based Internet company About.com. He has been involved in theatre professionally at various times as a writer, director, house manager, journalist, photographer and administrator. He was an amateur actor for many years and is currently a board member of a receiving theatre and the artistic director of KG Productions, a small-scale production company.

Sylvia Read and **William Fry (Performing in Churches)** have been on the road together as Theatre Roundabout for nearly forty years, giving more than 3,800 performances in theatres, arts centres, halls, schools and universities, but mainly in churches and cathedrals in Europe and the United States. For two years they worked as joint directors of Radius, the Religious Drama Society of Great Britain. Both are published playwrights, and their book *Christian Theatre: a Handbook for Church Groups* (Eyre & Spottiswoode) is a foundation text for the Wesley Seminary in Washington, DC.

Robert Reed (Tax and Accounting) joined the Inland Revenue in 1968 and was part of the specially selected team which formed the first London Special Office in 1976 where he worked as an investigator concentrating on the tax issues relating to the entertainment industry. He left the Revenue in 1987 to join the media and entertainment group of Touche Ross (now Deloitte & Touche). Robert has since advised on major theatre productions around the world, including in the West End, on Broadway, in Canada, Germany and Australia, as well as smaller theatre groups in the UK.

John Scowen (Performing at Festivals) has been involved in the amateur theatre for over twenty years. He has been a director, an actor, and has undertaken many of the jobs involved in putting on a show. Over the past ten years he has taken an active role in drama festivals and runs the Thurrock Drama Festival. He is the chairman of Thurrock Arts Council and an executive committee member of the National Drama Festival Association (NDFA).

Clare Simpson (Fund-raising and Marketing) is development director for the Royal Lyceum Theatre Companies in Edinburgh, one of the city's major producing theatre company. She holds an MBA and has been working with both professional and amateur theatre groups for many years. Her current professional remit includes fund-raising, education and generating audiences.

Liz Tomlin and **Steve Jackson (Accessibility).** Liz is a research fellow in performing arts at Manchester Metropolitan University and is co-director with **Steve Jackson** of Open Performance Centre Limited. The company provides opportunities for local communities to get involved in the performing arts through training courses, work placements and participatory productions. They also co-direct the professional touring company Point Blank, which is based at the Open Performance Centre, and conduct research into contemporary performance training in association with Manchester Metropolitan University.

Harry Venning (Illustrations) provides two weekly newspaper cartoon strips: *Hamlet* for the *Stage* and *Clare in the Community* for the *Guardian.*

Bob Wearn (Musicians) trained at Dartington College of Arts and was a peripatetic violin teacher in Swindon, Wiltshire, before moving to Leeds as the Musicians' Union's north-east district organiser. He was appointed assistant general secretary with special responsibility for live engagements in 1997.

Foreword

You don't have to be a Judi Dench or a Kenneth Branagh to gain enjoyment and a sense of achievement from personal participation in theatre. Many thousands of ordinary people scurry home from work, change their clothes and sometimes go without dinner in order to get to their local village hall, community centre or, for the fortunate ones, their own amateur theatre building. There they rehearse month after month for one or more nights a week in order to present works of drama, opera or music theatre to their local communities. In the background even more thousands are busy managing local theatre groups, making and sewing costumes, building sets, designing and rigging lighting, making props, arranging front-of-house and bar rotas, organising box offices and undertaking the million other essential tasks that are needed to ensure that a short run enthrals a paying audience.

The whole process can be exhilarating and the satisfaction on the last night can be enormous. It is even greater when, from the beginning, a company has confidence that everything that needs to be done has been done with care and efficiency. But it's one thing to put on a show and quite another to set up a company that will, perhaps, produce many. Books abound on costume, make-up, lighting design, prop making and the whole range of practical activities involved in putting on a show. However, until now there has been no single guide combining artistic and practical advice designed to take you through the whole process of organising an amateur theatre company. This handbook will help you to follow correct procedures, recognise and avoid pitfalls and ensure that whether you want to set up a drama club or stage a one-off performance at any type of venue, all your decisions are not only practicable but also within the various legal requirements affecting public presentation of dramatic work.

Keith Arrowsmith's handbook, wittily illustrated by Harry Venning, leads the beginner comprehensively through the process and reminds the experienced practitioner of the regulations which need to be observed in order to produce amateur theatre with a professional attitude. It answers such vital questions as: *Do you really have to spray Aunt Muriel's Edwardian chaise longue, borrowed for your play, with fireproofing material? How do you raise the last £500 needed to present an open-air show at a local venue and what health and safety requirements must you fulfil? Why can't you make a video of your show for sale to the cast? Who owns the copyright if you make a sound recording of your Gilbert & Sullivan production? How do you make sure that adequate insurance is available for all working on a show as well as the equipment used and the audience?*

I foresee the handbook, which is informative, comprehensive and highly readable, becoming a definitive reference book not only for amateur theatre enthusiasts but also for many professional theatres. I have no hesitation at all in commending it to all who delight in amateur theatre.

Tom Williams
Chairman
Central Council for Amateur Theatre

Introduction

Bringing a live show to an audience can be a magical experience. From a simple classical monologue to the most complex modern musical, rich rewards can be gained from being involved in the art of performance. Of the thousands of people experiencing this thrill on stage in any week, there are hundreds of people behind the scenes, making sure that the production is 'all right on the night'. But the process of putting a show on stage can be complicated. There can be setbacks at every turn, and the potential for disaster is sometimes too much to contemplate.

It can be a costly exercise to present a play or musical, and breaking even is not guaranteed. Competition is high for limited subsidies or sponsorship, with many funders demanding more in return for their support. Participants and audiences are in short supply, with theatre competing with an ever increasing list of other leisure activities. Some costs are not monetary, for the stage is an unfamiliar environment, where accidents often occur: it is surprisingly easy to fall off a stage into the orchestra pit.

It is also a field in which reputation is important. A public performance exposes the skill and creativity of the artist and the organisation to scrutiny. Every person's input for each show could enhance or damage that reputation. Performance is therefore a team activity, which could easily be let down by the weakest link.

Despite these stresses and strains, the performing arts continue to attract performers, producers and supporters. Can all this effort be justified? London's West End proves that theatre can be big business. A long-running musical can earn millions of pounds. But most who have chosen the performing arts as their profession do not achieve large financial rewards. Other motivating factors must be at work, which are as relevant to the amateur stage as the professional production. Quality need not vary between the two. Traditionally, audiences expected less of the amateur theatre, but this is changing. If an amateur group is to meet the growing expectations of its paying public, it must recognise this shift and endeavour to achieve rising standards.

At the same time, the rights and responsibilities of the individual are changing. European, national and local regulations all apply to live performances. The number and complexity of these rules is increasing. It is tempting to ignore the current situation, or pretend that 'red tape' does not apply to the non-professional theatre. However, these controls are put in place in an attempt to regulate competing interests and to limit the risk of significant harm. It is dangerous to ignore them, especially as we continue to move towards a blame-led culture. Conversely, there are areas of live performance where there are no rules or regulations. These are steeped in theatre-lore and traditions which may go unquestioned. Here the challenge is to sort the good practice from the bad.

It is often difficult, especially for smaller groups, to ensure that there are sufficient volunteers to attend to the less glamorous aspects of theatre production. Keeping abreast of the latest developments may be seen as a luxury which cannot be afforded. Yet, any group that does not keep up to date will find itself in trouble sooner rather than later.

This handbook is for everyone who is involved in amateur theatre. It is based on the principle that 'amateur' need not mean 'amateurish'. Although much of what is set out in the following sections will be relevant to the professional theatre, the reverse is not necessarily true. Many sections will also be relevant to practitioners and managers of live dance or music. Whether you are a seasoned practitioner, or new to the world of the performing arts, I hope that this handbook can provide you with relevant, practical guidance.

TERMS USED IN THIS HANDBOOK

I am painfully aware that lawyers often use language in a peculiar manner. Sometimes we use a term in a technical way that is different to its everyday meaning. I have made every effort to eliminate any superfluous legalese, but what remains is unavoidable and is explained in the Glossary on pages 267–73.

In general, I use the term 'group' to mean any number of people who have come together to stage a show. 'Show' means a play, musical or other live dramatic performance.

THE SECTIONS OF THE HANDBOOK

1 **Performance** concentrates on specific performance situations that can take place in many different settings, with their own particular concerns. This section also provides a useful introduction to the planning and rehearsal processes.
2 **The Show** takes you step by step through the planning processes, from initial idea to the last-night party. You will become familiar with the roles and responsibilities of the producers, actors, backstage crew and front-of-house managers.
3 **Management** explains the duties and obligations of the people who are responsible for the production. This will help you run a successful amateur dramatic organisation.
4 **Reference Section** provides additional information and resources for all aspects covered in this handbook.

NOTE

The guide has been written specifically for amateur theatre in Great Britain. The text refers to the law of England and Wales. Where Scottish law is materially different, this is highlighted. Although the book aims to provide a thorough introduction to this subject, it does not give a full statement of the law, nor does it reflect any changes after 1 July 2001. It is no substitute for professional advice. Hyperlinks and other updated material is available on www.athb.co.uk

Keith Arrowsmith
Sheffield 2001

1 Performance

Performing in Schools
Peter Lathan

PLANNING

Obviously, first choose your show. But what is perhaps not so obvious is the fact that, no matter whether it is one written specially for students or a mainstream show, you are going to have to pay a copyright licence fee, unless the copyright has expired. There is no special dispensation from the copyright regulations for schools or their productions. You must obtain permission from the rights holders *before rehearsals start.* Even if your production is to take place in front of a non-paying audience, you must still obtain permission – and it is more than likely that you will still have to pay a fee. See pages 83–97 for copyright rules.

However, it is worth making it clear that this is to be a school's performance, as there might be some discount on the fee. And if your hall or wherever you perform is small, it is worth mentioning that too: there is usually a discount for small venues. My school's hall only holds 200 and that has often given us discount in the past.

Buy (or hire) your scripts. Do not photocopy without permission – it is a breach of copyright.

Where is all this money going to come from? Scripts to buy, royalties to pay, props to make, scenery to build – it is all going to cost. Borrow it! No, not a personal loan from the bank! Get the head to loan you the money from the school fund. Work out how much it is all going to cost, add a hundred quid, and that is how much to ask for. Prepare a budget. An example is set out on page 72. The show is going to cost £X because of a, b, c, d, etc. However, you expect that you will have an audience of Y: N students in the cast will bring in a minimum of N adults and, say, N children. Then add other students from the school, other friends, other adults to bring the total up to Y. Divide the cost, £X, by Y and you have an average seat price – £Z. Sort that into a price for adults which is twice that for children. There's your business plan! The head can see that money is not being thrown away. Of course, you aim to have more in the audience than this, because you want to make a profit over and above the £100 contingency you have set.

But do insist on having control of the profit. It will remain in the school fund account, of course – no head will allow a school account to be controlled by an ordinary member of staff! – but it should be kept in a notional fund within that account and you can make the decisions as to how that money is to be spent. Mainly, of course, it will be 'seed money' for the next production, but you might want to buy equipment. School shows can be profitable. Our production of *Little Shop of Horrors* cost about £450, but we took almost £1,300 – just over £800 profit. We bought a couple of superb shotgun microphones out of that.

You are going to need a public entertainment licence from the local authority, so you need to contact them very early in the proceedings, particularly if this is your first school production. See pages 132–4 for details. You may need to arrange a visit from a fire officer who will lay down certain conditions regarding the number of audience members allowed, fire exits and signage, where seating can be placed, type of emergency lighting, and so on. You must comply with all their requirements as they have the power to shut the show down, even in the middle of a performance. I find that friendly school secretaries are usually willing to help with the paperwork. And make sure you have the caretaker on your side, for s/he may have to be involved in the preparation of the hall to meet the standards required by the fire officer.

And are you going to play recorded music before your show or during the interval? You need licences for that too, from the Performing Rights Society and Phonographic Performance Limited. See page 174 for more details. Some schools benefit from a licence

Get the head to loan you some money from the school fund.

taken out by the LEA to cover schools, community centres and so on, but you will need to check to see if that licence applies to your school.

GETTING THE SHOW ON THE ROAD

The most important thing to remember about working with students is that they will do their best to live up to your expectations, so if your expectations are low, then you will get a low standard. I was appalled on one occasion, when watching a colleague directing a play, to see that she had only two instructions to give: 'Speak up' and 'Put some expression into your voice'. She ended up with a production in which the actors spoke loudly (or shouted) and said their lines as if they were reading them from a book. They stood rigidly, or danced from foot to foot, and quite clearly hadn't the faintest idea what to do with their hands. When they moved, they shuffled, or strolled, or simply got from point A to point B as quickly as possible. I asked her later – and yes, I *was* trying to catch her out – how they had dealt with the emotional subtext. 'Oh, we didn't do that,' she said. 'They're just students.'

Children can produce first-class work. They can act as well as any adult. They can convince you and they can move you. All you have got to do is make it clear you expect it of them – and show them how to do it. I have directed *Steel Magnolias* with sixteen-year-olds, and there was not a dry eye in the house. I have directed *Educating Rita* with sixteen-year-olds, and the audience lapped it up. The last production I did before writing this was Claire Dowie's *Adult Child/ Dead Child* with two seventeen-year-old girls, and when they walked into the foyer afterwards, the audience burst into spontaneous applause. Never, never ever underestimate what children, whether aged seven or seventeen, can do in performance.

Recently we took a production of *The Wizard of Oz* to Germany. The company was made up mainly of students from years seven and eight. We were booked to play three performances in three different venues. Each was completely different from the others: significantly different sizes of stage; entrances in different places – in one the only entrance was stage left, in another, stage right, in the third they could enter from both sides. In the one with the entrance on stage left, the dressing room – the only one, and it was tiny! – opened straight on to the stage, so they had to change their costumes in total darkness. They took these differences in their stride and you would have thought that they had actually rehearsed the show on each stage. How do we get children to do this? The keywords are *understanding* and *confidence*: without them, you will get nowhere.

DEVELOPING THE CONCEPT, AUDITIONS AND REHEARSALS

For me the beginning is quite some time before I start working with the students. For our major productions, we start working on the show in January, right at the start of the spring term, and perform just before Easter. My own work on it, however, begins in early December. And that work is developing the *concept* of the production.

The concept is my interpretation of the show. Take our production of *Toad of Toad Hall*, for instance. For me, the weasels and ferrets and stoats – the Wild Wooders – represent the dark side of human nature, which lies just below our civilised surface. In fact, to save Toad Hall, Toad's friends, Badger, Mole and Ratty, have to behave like the Wild Wooders. This was the basic concept which I wanted to get across to the audience, so I staged the play in such a way as to suggest this, right from the start.

The audience sat on three sides of the stage and the whole auditorium represented the Wild Wood. There were trees in the auditorium, the walls were covered with leaves and, as the audience entered, the place was lit with a green light and the Wild Wooders scuttled around, popping their heads up and hissing. When Badger and the others were forced to adopt Wild-Wooder tactics, the light on the stage, which until then had been warm, gradually took on a green tinge, so that, in the wild celebrations which followed the victory, the stage was beginning to look like the Wild Wood.

All this was worked out before we began rehearsals. It had to be, otherwise the subsequent stages of the production would have had no real focus. And the first of these stages is casting.

I do not audition. We need to mould the students into a unit, working together and totally trusting each other, and starting off by putting them in deliberate competition against each other is hardly the way to achieve this. It might work for adults – it might be the only way – but it does not work for students. Instead, I do workshops built around the show in some way – and these ways are not always obvious. If the show is *Godspell*, for instance, which is very much an ensemble piece, then at least one full workshop will focus on the ability to work together, using a series of exercises:

> Crowd everyone into a big bunch and lay a rope on the floor around them. They are on an island and, as the tide comes in, that island will shrink: they must ensure that everyone remains safe. They step off the island and walk around it, while I shrink the size of the space within the rope. On the command 'Now!', they must all get on to the island. No one must be abandoned to the sea. The island continues to shrink: they continue to try to save everyone.

There will also be exercises which concentrate on text:

> I use a couple of lines from *A Midsummer Night's Dream* for this, but you can choose your own. The lines are 'O spite! O hell! I see you all are bent to set against me for your merriment'. They have to say the lines in various tones of voice: angrily, sadly, as loudly as they can, as softly, and so on. Then they have to sing them in a style of their choosing. Many will choose rap (well, it is dead easy), so you accept it, then do it again in a different style.

> A fun exercise is to give them a couple of verses of 'I am the very model of a modern major-general' from *The Pirates of Penzance* and have them speak them as quickly as possible.

In twos, get them to hold an (almost) intelligible conversation using only the word 'blah' (or 'spam' if you are a Monty Python fan).

At some point it is a good idea, in groups of a suitable size, to give them a short scene from the play and see what they do with it. I watch them carefully all the time, assessing and comparing what they do to my preconceived ideas about character and performance. And of course I also take into account what I know of their abilities from previous shows and from drama lessons. Once I have a fair idea in my mind about who should do what, I consult my musical director to make sure that my choices can sing the character's songs, if there are any. Working like this, they are already, without realising it, working on their performances in the show.

Before going any further, let us look at the legal side. Do you need to have the parents' permission for children to be involved in a school production? Obviously you do, but it does not have to be written, although you may feel safer that way. See page 108 for details. What you must do, whether in written form or verbally, is let the students and, through them, the parents, know exactly what it is they are letting themselves in for. This means you must give an indication of how much time you will require them to give to the production, when rehearsals will take place (particularly if you do any at weekends, during holidays – say, half-term – or at night, when they have to return to school), and when the production will be, how many nights it will run for, what time you expect it to finish, and so on. And just to cover myself, I will always state under what circumstances I reserve the right to remove someone from the cast.

A few years ago, we had a rehearsal on the Sunday before opening on the Tuesday, as we always do. The crew and I spent the morning setting up the lighting for this crucial technical rehearsal later in the day. One of our dancers was involved in a local amateur operatic group's show, which was to be performed three weeks after ours. They had a rehearsal at the same time as our tech. Her mother wrote to me saying that she, the mother, had decided that her daughter should go to the amateur operatic group's rehearsal. I wrote back saying that I had decided that if she missed our rehearsal, she was out of the show. Mother wrote back saying that it was her decision and so it was unfair for the girl to be punished. I replied that they had both agreed to the conditions when we began rehearsals, and that was that. I was not prepared to discuss the matter any further. The girl did not come, so I made the decision to remove her from the cast. Harsh? Perhaps, but giving in would have meant sending signals which said that our production was not important.

So, casting is complete and we come to the first reading, where the parts are given out and we read through the play. Sometimes casting can cause problems, with students – and their parents – being convinced that they should have had part A, not B, or should have had a main role, not just be part of the chorus. You simply have to have the courage of your convictions and stick by your choice: do not weaken in the face of parental pressure or you will never be able to make an unchallenged decision again.

I always preface the read-through with a brief sketch of each character as I see them, but I make it clear that this is not the final picture, as I expect actors to come up with their own interpretations and ideas. The first reading also serves as an opportunity to explain the basic concept and to encourage the students to think how their performance can contribute to it. And before you start thinking, 'But these are just students: they won't be able to do that,' I can assure you that they can – and do. When we were working on *Little Shop of Horrors*, this was the point at which we established that the piece was to be played straight, with no attempts to send it up, and, in the reading, it was possible to nip any tendency to do so in the bud.

Next comes what has to be the most boring part of any production, the blocking, or setting moves. It is important at this point to make it absolutely clear that these moves are not set in stone: they are simply a starting point and many, if not most, will probably change as characters develop and the cast's understanding of the play grows. I do not even write them down. The cast do, of course, because they need to remember next time, but I always insist on moves being written lightly in pencil, so they can be easily rubbed out and replaced. My students have learned over the years that a pencil and rubber are essential tools of the actor's trade.

We try to get blocking over with as quickly as possible: it is a real strain on the cast having to keep silent for a couple of hours while I move bodies around the stage, but they know they have to do it.

At this point it is worth mentioning how frequently we rehearse and how long rehearsals are. I know many schools that rehearse for two terms or even a whole school year. We do not: our rehearsal period is eight weeks, give or take. That means we rehearse three or four nights a week, with the other nights, plus lunchtimes and breaks, taken up with music rehearsals. Initially rehearsals are an hour and a half, but after four weeks we go to two hours and might even overrun that. It is demanding, both on the cast and on me, but I find it the best way to work. In a long rehearsal period the students get stale and rehearsals can become a bore. In the short period that we use, there is no time for boredom to set in.

Then the real work begins! Rehearsals are not just a matter of going over lines and moves. Of course, that is how they begin, but they should include much more than that. I have said that students can act as well as adults, but they have to be taught to do so. Some of this teaching begins before you embark on a production: my normal drama club meetings (once a week for an hour and a half) are aimed towards just that. We do voice exercises, body-control exercises, concentration exercises, text exercises – using improvised and text-based work – and all have one aim: to teach the students to act.

Incidentally, I always believe that those who get the best results out of students are those who have acting experience themselves. If all else fails – and you need to adopt a number of different strategies – you can fall back on showing what you want and getting the actor to mimic your performance. It is far from the best way of working, but at times it is the only one.

As you progress through your rehearsals, problems will surface. A move looks wrong. Begin to find the solution by putting the onus on the actor. Ask, 'Does that feel right?' If the answer is 'No', then ask, 'What do you think you should do?' However, if the answer is 'I don't know', then you have a problem which needs to be sorted there and then. Ask, 'Why did you do that?' And make it clear that the answer you require is *not* 'You told me to'. Get him/her to think about the character's motivation, his/her emotional state. In many cases this should be enough and the actor will come up with a more suitable alternative. If not, further questioning or even an improvised scene may be the way to elicit a suitable response. As a last resort – and if you have to do this, then your actor probably is not quite up to the part – demonstrate.

Or you might find that the actor knows exactly what to do and understands why it should be done, but is unable, for one reason or another, to do it. Then it is up to you to devise some way of overcoming the block. When I was rehearsing Anouilh's *Antigone* – incidentally a great play for students to do, for they really do relate to it – the boy who played Haemon could not handle the scene where he and Antigone embraced. He was, I think, a little too young – although I have to say that I have worked with adults who have found love scenes difficult – and was stiff and uncomfortable. In normal life we are very careful about whom we allow within our private space, but an actor must be comfortable with anyone getting so close. So I simply stopped the rehearsal and sent everyone except Antigone and Haemon away, because I knew we had a time-consuming problem on our hands.

What we did was a series of exercises which would help him overcome this block. We began by the two of them standing a couple of steps apart, staring into each other's eyes for a few minutes. Move closer: repeat. Closer still: repeat. Take her hand: repeat. Hands on each other's shoulders: repeat. We did not force it. We tried other exercises too: they walked around the room hand-in-hand but with arms at full stretch. Then closer. Closer. And so on, until eventually he was able to relax into the scene. The girl was very supportive – she was a more experienced actress – and, when eventually he was able to do it, they spontaneously hugged each other. It took a long time, but it was not wasted time because from then on the scene looked completely natural. And no, they did not start going out with each other: they were just good friends!

I have also spent upwards of half an hour on one line. It sometimes happens that an actor simply cannot get exactly the right tone and we need to work to get it right. As always, the last resort is imitating my performance, but it is far better if it comes from within the actor. A useful way of achieving this is to run the scene exactly as it was rehearsed but with the actor who is having the problem speaking aloud the character's feelings. They may find it difficult the first time, but persevere: it is worth it. Sometimes a scene seems to be wrong for no obvious reason, and the 'speaking the thoughts/feelings' exercise can solve that problem.

Sometimes a good discussion can do the show a world of good. I remember doing an extract from *Richard III* with three very experienced sixteen-year-old girls and our first rehearsal after the blocking was spent in deep discussion about the scene, the characters and their motivation. When, at the next rehearsal, we began to go through the scene, it needed very little work: they had thought it through and their acting technique was good enough to set a high standard. All that was needed was refinement.

Finally, there is what I call the 'babble' rehearsal. This is a way of fixing the lines in actors' minds. We simply rush through a scene, babbling the lines and running the moves. Occasionally we will do it without the moves: it really does concentrate the mind on the words.

When students take part in shows outside school — dance troupes in pantomimes, for instance — there are very strict rules about how much time they are allowed to spend not just performing or rehearsing, but actually being in the theatre. See pages 105-6 for details. Although those rules do not apply for school productions, you still have to be sensible. If their participation in the school show starts to impact on the time they have for their homework, you will soon have teachers complaining. If rehearsals finish around five thirty, most of the students should be home for six. Does that leave them sufficient time for homework? Of course it does! It may not give them sufficient time for homework *and* their social lives, but they have to be made aware of the fact that their social lives will have to suffer. The vast majority accept that. In fact, the rehearsals become part of their social lives.

THE TECHNICAL AND DRESS REHEARSALS

As far as possible, I like the tech side to be handled by the students. I spend a lot of time training those who are interested in sound and lighting so that they know the systems they have to use inside out. Do remember that all health and safety rules must be observed. In fact, you have to be doubly careful when working with students. Procedures must be very tight and all risks reduced to an absolute minimum – where an adult may take a chance, a child must not be allowed to do so, even if the risk of something going wrong is slight. Health and safety rules and regulations are outlined on pages 151–8: abide by them.

Every show needs a final rehearsal so that all of the technical aspects can be sorted out. There is one thing you can be sure of: no matter how well rehearsals were going, everything will fall apart at the tech and, by the end, you and the students will be feeling totally depressed. Now is the time to be understanding and supportive. Tell them you expected it to be bad. Remind them that they had been fine before. Lift them.

Finally we come to the dress. There is no truth in the old superstition that a bad dress rehearsal means a good show – a bad dress rehearsal means a bad dress rehearsal and that's all. However, I am always happier if the dress does not go smoothly, and the reason is simple: students play on their nerves. Tell them they *can* do it but need that extra effort, more concentration and greater energy, and then let the adrenalin do its work.

A tip: if you can get some school time for rehearsal, grab it with both hands. I have always managed to do so, partially because the argument that the students have given up so much of their own time that they deserve some of the school's is quite cogent, and partially because I will nag and nag until I get what I want! I do not, however, put an extra burden on colleagues by asking for cover for my lessons. I take my classes into the rehearsals, for two reasons: first, it sells tickets; second, it shows drama classes just what rehearsal really means. They are learning by watching.

But how do you deal with other staff who complain about taking students from their lessons? Usually there will not be many, but there will be some. If they are talking about students who are coming close to external exams, then you will probably have to give way gracefully, although I have been known to promise that the students will make up the work – and I have sat with them over lunchtimes till they do. But if it is any other year group, rely upon your persuasive powers/sarcasm/bad temper – whatever will work best with the individual.

THE PERFORMANCES

You should not have to worry about ticket or programme sales, or organising the box office or the ushers, or selling refreshments. You will not have the time, and you certainly will not have the energy. Get some other member of staff to act as house manager, but it is your responsibility to make sure that the house manager is aware of the school's obligations under the terms of the public performance licence. Legally, your hall ceases to be a school hall and becomes a theatre for the duration of the performances.

CONCLUSION

Has all this put you off? Do you feel that it is all just too demanding of your time and energy? Are you thinking at this moment that you want to have a life? If so, then don't do it. But if, recognising all the disadvantages and demands that are going to be made on you, you still want to go ahead, go for it. The buzz you will get is tremendous and you and the students will see a totally different side of each other. And I know this seems odd in terms of the teacher/pupil situation, but you will be making friends too. I have many very valued friends who were once pupils who appeared in my shows, from the two seventeen-year-old girls who were in my production of *Adult Child/Dead Child*, through the twenty-five-year-old who is now working in our local theatre, to the girl who appeared in my very first school production back in 1967 and who is now fifty!

Performance by Youth Groups

Stuart Hawkes and Roger Hill

INTRODUCTION

The term 'youth theatre' has been used in the years since the Second
World War to denote the creative use of young people's spare time
through the medium of theatre and drama. The activity has grown
out of school drama, enlightened amateur theatre and community
drama initiatives, but is not now tied to any single institutional
allegiance and involves theatrical performances created by many
different groupings of young people. As the number of youth theatres
in the United Kingdom has increased steadily since the early 1980s to
about 700, there has been a huge growth in the numbers of young
people involved and considerable development of youth theatre-
related work in many areas of cultural activity. Eleven–twenty-year-
olds are the most active participants. Drama groups for the unemployed, run on fundamentally similar lines to youth theatre groups
in response to the high youth unemployment of the 1980s, enlarged
the age range which now extends to thirty years and older. Youth
group leaders are from a wide range of professional backgrounds, but
primarily education, theatre and youth work.

In the summer of 1956 Michael Croft undertook a production of
Shakespeare's *Henry V* with a group of former pupils from Alleyn's
School in Dulwich where he had been teaching. His project grew in
scope and reputation, despite many struggles for official recognition
and funding, and in 1961 was given the title 'National Youth
Theatre'. By its thirtieth anniversary season in 1986, also the year of

Croft's death, it had established a solid tradition of multiple productions during its summer season, related outreach work and international tours attracting young people from all over the country.
Now known as the 'National Youth Theatre of Great Britain', it
continues to flourish under its current artistic director, Edward
Wilson.

Of the youth theatre developments inspired by Michael Croft's
work, many also took the form of a summer school drawing on
young people from a wide geographical area, for example the long-
established Manchester Youth Theatre. In the 1970s county youth
theatres were established by local education authorities in places like
Leicestershire, Devon and Northumberland, and, more recently,
comprehensive youth theatre development which emphasises year-
round work rather than the summer school format has been initiated
by education authorities in Wigan, Nottingham and elsewhere.
Meanwhile, National Youth Theatre summer schools have been set
up in Scotland, Wales and Northern Ireland. Another offshoot from
the National Youth Theatre was the annual National Festival of
Youth Theatre. This week-long event was first held in 1977 in
Leicestershire and was sponsored predominantly by education
authorities. It was last held in 1986, but there are now many regional
youth theatre festivals and gatherings held each year throughout the
country.

Much of the early proliferation of youth theatre work occurred in
the areas of education and extra-curricular activity. By the 1970s,
however, a number of regional repertory theatres had established
their own groups that often grew and flourished through contact
with theatre professionals. Now, with Arts Council encouragement,
many repertory theatres sponsor such activities as part of their policy.
Since the 1980s various local government departments concerned
with recreation and youth work have realised that youth theatre has
much to offer young people in an era of (sometimes enforced) leisure.
Increasingly, therefore, youth and community centres have sought to
add drama groups to their widening range of activities. It is, however,
generally true that, whatever its source of support, youth theatre has

owed its rather ad hoc growth to a number of committed and hard-working individuals.

In the work of a number of groups, youth theatre is essentially a non-political activity without an apparent ideology. However, there is a recent tendency for both process and product to be concerned with the potentially political issues of racism, sexism, bullying, disadvantage and with special-needs groups. Some leaders now concentrate on handing over responsibility for the theatre-making process to their groups, an empowering act which is also essentially political. Funding is, of course, another sensitive subject, and the most appropriate means to develop youth theatre work is currently being debated by proponents of centralised funding for 'quality' projects and advocates of a wide network of well-supported local groups which meet regularly all year round. The idea is gaining acceptance that both need support and that local and national bodies have a part to play in sustaining them. At the same time the nationwide network of groups is still far from complete and the National Association of Youth Theatres (NAYT) has dedicated its work to this development. The disparity in provision of youth theatre around the country has been countered by development projects in rural areas and large estates on the edge of cities. This has seemed to redress the unfortunate erosion of support to existing groups from local authorities affected by government strictures on public spending.

In Great Britain in the 1990s youth theatre has responded to changing social and economic conditions in a number of ways. An increasing national emphasis on training initiatives has offered an opportunity for the movement to consider the nature and structure of its professionalism at a national level and to create initiatives for skills development and accredited leadership courses. One landmark event of this process was the National Training Conference organised in 1991 in Sheffield by NAYT. Many youth theatre groups have also taken advantage of their capacity for distinctive and original work by moving into cross-art-form projects, encouraged in many cases by NAYT support schemes like New Initiatives and Fusions of

Excellence. This has reinforced youth theatre's role as a medium with potential for considerable experimentation.

SETTING UP A YOUTH THEATRE

There is currently no legislation specifically concerning the setting-up and development of youth theatre. These groups only have to comply with the standard rules and procedures which all other amateur theatre groups have to abide by. So why might you, as an amateur group or individual, want to set up a youth theatre? For many in the field it might be about ensuring the continuation of your group. For others there might be young members who are under-utilised. The 'why' very much sets the agenda. But beware: involving young people might not be as straightforward as you imagined. Before we go any further it might be worth considering the 'why' question in more detail.

- What is it that you are going to provide for your youth theatre members?
- Are they to participate in a skills workshop programme, or is the aim of the group simply to produce plays?
- Are you going to hold auditions?
- What will you charge?
- Where will the members come from?
- What will their age range be?
- Is your venue suitable?
- Who will work with the group?
- Do you have adequate insurance?
- How will the group be constituted?
- Who will support the group and who might provide help, advice and funding?

There is little doubt that young people's involvement in creative activity is a good thing. At its best, it builds their confidence and self-esteem, it allows them to explore issues and create responses to the world around them, it allows them to take risks within a safe and structured environment, it allows them to succeed. At its worst, it can do just the opposite, with young people developing a dismissive and negative attitude to the arts. A young person's first experience needs to be a positive one otherwise they will not come back for a second, and why should they? Therefore, if you are going to set up a youth theatre, you have a responsibility to ensure that you provide the best opportunities that you can.

So who is going to come to your youth theatre? The average youth theatre in the UK has eighty members. The average young person involved is aged fifteen, female and her parents are not averse to watching theatre. The majority have waiting lists. If you want to extend the opportunity to a wider range of young people then you will need to be proactive in attracting them to your youth theatre.

A good starting point might be your local senior schools. Speak to the drama teachers there; they will have regular contact with young people who may wish to get involved. Teachers may also know of other local groups or what activities their pupils already take part in. The local authority's youth service might also be worth a call. Youth workers are constantly looking for new opportunities for their young people to get involved in. Think where young people are already being worked with, you might be able to offer a group a taster workshop.

WHAT ARE YOU GOING TO DO WITH THEM?

One of the main differences between the funded and non-funded sector is their approach to skills and group development. Many youth theatres in the funded sector have annual programmes that centre on skills development and the creation of devised work. For the majority in the non-funded sector, the focus is on yearly or twice-yearly productions.

In a workshop programme the emphasis is on developing the creative skills of the individual and their ability to work as a function-ing member of a team. Workshop programmes might include specialist areas such as comedy, or concentrate on improvisation, voice or movement. Most of these workshops will have a strong emphasis on group work, encouraging participants to challenge while equipping them to be challenged. Many youth theatres will not even consider taking a group through to performance until they have been through these processes.

For many in the funded sector, youth theatre means devised performances. Unfortunately, for many, this decision has been made purely on funding terms and has led to the slightly disparaging and often unjustified tag of 'issue-based youth theatre'. This may result in lifeless performances centring on drugs, alcohol, sexual health, bullying, etc., where the emphasis is on the issue rather than on the quality of the theatre. But devised performances allow young people to have a voice. For them to create something that is theirs gives meaning to their world. Devised performances allow the group to work to its strengths and allow the participants to base their actions on their own experiences.

Another advantage of the devised performance is the removal of the need for auditions, as the piece is made to fit the group. Auditioning is a key issue for many youth theatres. Good sight readers are not always good actors and, equally, those who do not have good literary skills can often be the best performers. Success at auditions requires confidence. If one of your aims is to increase the confidence of your group, rejection might not be your best starting point. If you do need to weed out numbers, a series of workshop auditions will identify the most committed.

Script selection is always going to be difficult. Finding a script that includes seventeen parts for women and three parts for men remains hard. Plays that avoid the need for liberal use of false grey hair are not always easy to come by. The result, unfortunately, is a proliferation of *Dracula Spectacular* and *Grease*. These are often disappointing in their results, since if you haven't got John Travolta in the cast, your production might not live up to the expectations of your group. One recent initiative called 'BT Connections' involved the Royal National Theatre commissioning a number of new scripts for performance by young people. During 2001, the National Association of Youth Theatre developed a virtual script bank, detailing recommended plays and details of groups that have performed them. The NAYT web site (www.nayt.org.uk) includes links to specialist publishers.

Running a youth theatre will incur costs: rent, heating, lighting and worker fees, as well as refreshments, costumes, licences and insurance. Someone has to pay. Of course, you would hope that if you perform, your audience will be happy to hand over their cash; however, there are no guarantees. Groups will often base their programme around the need to generate sizeable audiences. The downside to this approach is that it often means selecting an old favourite. Unfortunately, the chances are high that a group down the road may have produced that same old favourite only last year. There will always be a difficult balance between artistic risk and box-office income.

Charges to young people vary across the country. The commercial sector may charge participants upwards of four pounds an hour for their Saturday morning session. Across the voluntary and amateur sectors charging is quite common. Costs vary between fifty pence and three pounds per session. Some youth theatres expect payment on a term-by-term basis; however, for young people from low-income families this can prove to be a barrier.

For the funded sector the question is slightly different. Many youth theatres that are in receipt of public funding do not necessarily need to charge their participants but choose to do so in order that the young people see value in the activity.

WHERE ARE YOU GOING TO WORK FROM?

The question of venue needs careful consideration. The first implication is cost. If you do not have your own building, where can you go? School buildings provide excellent facilities for drama and are often available after hours for community use. Equally, local authorities often provide space within youth clubs, community centres or adult education blocks. Community-based groups should expect to pay a reduced rate for local authority space.

It might be useful to consider that young people are often territorial. If you use a school building, it might be difficult to attract young people from different schools; if you use a youth centre, regular users may take an interest in someone else using their space. Though church halls are physically suitable, many young people may not be comfortable with the notion of working in one. Your front room is not a suitable place for youth theatre activity.

When you have found your space a simple risk assessment is always worthwhile. Details appear on page 153. Make sure that your group understands the fire procedures and make sure that you take a register and contact numbers for parents/carers in case of emergency. Having a qualified first aider on site would be a good idea. At this stage you should also check out your need for insurance. Further details of the types of cover you may need are on pages 237-9.

YOUTH WORKERS

So now you've got a group and somewhere to meet and an idea about a programme of activities but who is going to work with the young people? The burning question that most parents would ask would concern the suitability of any adult workers or volunteers. Working with young people is not the same as working with adults. Young people can be very vulnerable and often appear to be more streetwise than they actually are. There have been enough stories in the media for us all to be aware of paedophiles and it would be naive if we were to imagine that the arts were somehow exempt. Recent legislation concerning, adults' appropriate relationships with young people in their charge has implications for the amateur and voluntary sector. It is not appropriate for youth theatre leaders to enter into relationships with members, even if they are beyond the age of consent. If you are employing someone to work with young people or are using volunteers they should be police checked. See pages 109–10 for details.

If you are using volunteers, what skills do they have? Art-form training is often provided locally; your local authority's cultural

Your front room is not a suitable place for youth theatre activity.

services department may wish to support a programme of amateur arts development. Youth service departments run youth work training courses for those who are looking to increase their skills in working with young people. NAYT run regular training events both regionally and nationally.

If you want to work with a professional writer, designer or director, your arts board will have a database of practitioners and can give you advice on how much you should expect to pay for their services. Alternatively, contact other youth theatres and ask whom they have worked with.

Support for your group is essential, especially if you are going to attempt to raise funds. Involving people in an advisory group or steering committee will allow you to make contact with key workers in the local authority and local community. This will not only give you the opportunity to pick their brains but also allows you to show that you are serious in your intent. Involving the local youth service, for example, will ensure that you are kept abreast of issues relating to young people, and a representative from cultural services could keep you up to date with arts development issues.

THE CONSTITUTION FOR A YOUTH THEATRE

In order to attract any form of public funding, including grants from the National Lottery, local grants, etc., you will need a written constitution and a bank account in the name of the group. Not only will each group need to decide how much the members will be involved in writing or directing each production, but the group will need to set down in the constitution which group members will take part in its management. Banks will not allow people under eighteen to be named on the mandate for cheque signing, and company law regulations do not allow child directors, but there is no reason why the members of the youth theatre cannot otherwise be involved in the management of the group: such involvement helps reinforce that the group belongs to its members.

By way of example, the Beck Youth Theatre, based in west

London, is an independent youth theatre company, which is funded entirely by fees, donations and ticket sales. First formed in 1987 by theatre management, it became an independent charity in 1992. Its written constitution clearly states that the group was formed to:

educate, and promote the education of, young people in the appreciation and practice of drama and the performance arts.

To enable the youth theatre to meet this objective, it has created five categories of membership:

Associate Membership is open to all persons in the age range 8 through 25, who support the aims and objects of the Society.

Junior Membership is open only to Associate Members who are aged 18 or under, and who, by means of interview and audition, can demonstrate their ability to learn, their willingness to take part in learning situations and live performance, and their commitment to the aims and objects of the Society.

Senior Membership is open only to Associate Members who are aged 18 years or older, and who, by means of interview and audition, can demonstrate their ability to learn, their willingness to take part in learning situations and live performance, and their commitment to the aims and objects of the Society.

Honorary Membership is exceptionally conferred upon persons who have been selected by the Committee of the Society for their particular services to the Society, or to the performing arts in general.

Friends Membership is open to all persons of any age who support the aims and objects of the Society. Only Junior, Senior and Honorary members may take part in any production.

Only members aged 18 or over, or the legal guardian of members under this age, may serve on the Management Committee. All members may attend general meetings, and those members who, on the date of the meeting, have achieved an age of 15 years or greater are entitled to vote on any decision.

Using different types of membership enables this group to have an organised structure which allows all members of the youth theatre to feel involved. However, simpler forms of constitution may be more appropriate, and advice is available from umbrella organisations.

STAGE SCHOOLS

There has been a long tradition of dance academies, which is being augmented by local and national stage schools. As in every other sector, there are good and bad examples of these organisations. Some are run on a franchise basis, which means that all local branches operate under a common name with a structure based on a central model. Using a franchise is a quick way of obtaining a reputation, but it may be expensive in the long run. If your group is considering a franchise agreement, take legal advice before making any long-term commitment.

If you are thinking about joining a stage school, try to gather information about the organisation before you commit to paying a term's fees. Most groups will be happy to allow you to meet the leaders and talk with other members and parents.

CONCLUSION

NAYT now receives over a thousand enquiries each year from young people, their parents, teachers and youth workers, looking for support and advice about youth theatre provision. Increasingly, they are receiving calls from those people running or thinking about setting up a youth theatre. These calls range from advice about fundraising and licences through to selecting a script or hiring a drama worker.

It sounds like a lot of work, and it is. But if we are to make opportunities available to young people then they should be good opportunities. Working with young people can be frustrating, tiring and nerve-racking. Equally, it can be challenging, energising and rewarding. Theatre processes are good for young people. If we put young people at the centre of the process, then we will make good youth theatre.

Performing in Churches

Sylvia Read and William Fry

INTRODUCTION

From its primitive beginnings theatre has been deeply rooted in religious ceremony. After each harvest early Achaean tribes showed their gratitude to the gods by singing and dancing ecstatically on the threshing floor, and these rituals may have been one of the influences on early Greek classical drama. Even today it is easy for us to recognise the devotional content in the imposing tragedies of Aeschylus, Euripides and Sophocles, but it comes as more of a surprise to learn that the cheek, smut and general knockabout of an Aristophanes comedy provided another vital element in the religious festivals of ancient Greece.

The clowns in the Roman circus carried on this irreverent tradition and, when the official religion of the empire was changed to Christianity, they expected to make the same sort of fun of baptism, communion and, of course, the clergy. The shocked Fathers of the Church soon put an end to all that and, in so doing, they left both drama and religion rather bereft.

Like lovers whose parents have forbidden them to meet, Church and theatre yearned for one another. After all, they had a natural affinity. Slowly and stiffly the priests began to unbend, and liturgy slid imperceptibly into action and dialogue. In some churches in the Middle Ages the vicar and curate would run up the aisle to the Easter Sepulchre like Peter and John when they heard the news of the Resurrection. Francis of Assisi introduced the Christmas crib, and in churches like St Mary's, Bury St Edmunds, the Rood Loft became a narrow stage to enact the Crucifixion.

In England the most remarkable development produced the medieval *Mystery Plays*, performed not in churches but out in the streets, thus providing a living link between the Christian faith and secular life. Every year, at the feast of Corpus Christi, which falls in early summer, the craft guilds, or *Mysteries*, as they were called, presented the complete Christian cycle from the creation of Adam and Eve to the Last Judgement. Each guild presented its own portion of the story. The carpenters would perform Noah and his ark, the nailers the Crucifixion, and so on. The scenes were presented on carts at varying points in the town and the performers dragged their scenery with them from one place to the next. By waiting in the market place or the town square, you could see the whole drama of Salvation acted out before you in the course of a single day.

In this way, the Bible became a living reality, and people grew up with a sense of familiarity about such characters as Cain and Abel, Mr and Mrs Noah, Abraham and Isaac, Mary and Joseph, John the Baptist and King Herod. They were no 'stained-glass' characters, nor were they acted with undue piety: they were alive with all their faults and often with a far from reverent sense of humour. For instance, Mrs Noah was presented as a gossipy elderly woman who wanted her tittle-tattling friends to come on to the ark with her; while Joseph, on hearing from Mary that the Angel had visited her once more, replied with trepidation, 'Not again, Mary!'

At the Reformation, theatre and Church were driven apart again. Robbed of dramatic warmth and colour, divine service grew more severe and formal. Freed from all religious constraints, plays tended to become violent and indecent. No wonder that many Christians began to regard the playhouse with horror. In the eighteenth century the Lord Chamberlain was given the task of protecting public morals from the corruption of the theatre, and he forbade any character in the Bible to be represented on the stage.

This second divorce persisted for hundreds of years, partly because more and more writers of quality began to write novels rather than plays. It may have been the influence of that great religious playwright, Henrik Ibsen, on authors like George Bernard Shaw, Arthur Wing Pinero, John Galsworthy and Henry Arthur Jones that awoke the need to bring religion back into the theatre. It needed an even greater revolution to bring plays back into the Church. Today, when every village has its nativity play, it is hard to realise how impossible that seemed a hundred years ago.

The breakthrough came when the Dean of Canterbury, George Bell, commissioned John Masefield to write a play to be performed in the cathedral. By modern standards, *The Coming of Christ* was intensely traditional, but it caused a sensation when it played to packed houses for four nights in 1928. The money raised from those audiences was used to found an annual festival at Canterbury, and when George Bell became Bishop of Chichester he appointed E. Martin Browne as the very first diocesan drama adviser.

Soon afterwards the Religious Drama Society of Great Britain (now known as Radius) was founded by Sir Francis Younghusband on his return from India, where he had been deeply impressed by colourful troupes travelling from village to village playing Hindu ritual drama. For over seventy years Radius has encouraged, advised and promoted amateur theatre in churches and for church organisations, and its members up and down the country have put on plays, sketches and even musicals in churches and cathedrals throughout Britain.

Year after year distinguished authors wrote plays for the Canterbury Festival, and in 1936 came T. S. Eliot's great classic, *Murder in the Cathedral,* which suddenly lifted religious drama to the status of world-class theatre. Directed by E. Martin Browne, the play transferred to the Duchess Theatre in the West End, and later went on to a season on Broadway. Since then it has been performed by amateurs and professionals in a great variety of churches, halls and theatres.

This success encouraged many other writers to write plays for presentation in churches. Charles Williams, Christopher Fry, Norman Nicholson, Ronald Duncan and many others wrote intellectual plays in elegant verse. When the fashion changed, more populist works – *Joseph and his Technicolor Dreamcoat, Godspell* and *Jesus Christ Superstar* took London by storm. After their long separation, theatre and Church rushed into one another's arms.

Today many churches encourage the use of drama. At our own church at Hampstead, for instance, there is a talented group who mainly perform modern plays, such as *A Man For All Seasons* by Robert Bolt and *Racing Demon* by David Hare. In many churches it is not uncommon for the services themselves to contain a playlet, sketch or even dance to illustrate a Christian theme.

Churches have also begun to support a few professional touring companies, some of which (like Riding Lights) have achieved considerable distinction. Our own company, Theatre Roundabout, which is a professional one, has for the past forty years presented plays and revues in churches and for church organisations. Life on this kind of circuit can be tough and not particularly lucrative, so most of the performers involved are dedicated and fairly young, and, as with most small-scale touring theatre, the turnover rate is high.

It would be rash to predict from this recent revival in religious drama that Church and theatre will live together happily ever after. The tensions still remain. Even such a transparently Christian play as Shaw's *St Joan* is intensely critical of the Church, and comedies are likely to be even more disturbing than tragedies. For churchgoers who want their Christianity to be strictly conventional and for theatregoers who prefer what they call 'pure entertainment', the questions raised by genuinely religious theatre will prove equally disturbing.

Nevertheless, playing in churches can be extremely worthwhile. For one thing, in spite of all the talk of dwindling congregations, the church still reaches a surprisingly wide cross-section of the community. Some statisticians claim that more people go to church than go to football matches. Many men and women from every kind of background and occupation come for the key moments of their lives – baptism, marriage and burial. In many small villages, the church is the only community building, and even in towns it is often a great deal more beautiful than most of the halls on offer. Besides, many churches are pregnant with atmosphere. Here, men and women have brought their joys and sorrows, have prayed for healing, have found forgiveness, have been heartened, inspired and

Performing in churches.

comforted. No wonder the building itself is alive with memories which can only enhance any piece of theatre performed there.

This atmosphere can create a sort of trampoline of emotion which can be tremendously helpful when performing. Recently we have been touring with our own adaptation of William Nicholson's *Shadowlands* round theatres and halls in Britain, on the Continent and in the USA, but it is in churches that the play seems to evoke the most intense response. Of course, it isn't easy to mount drama in a church. Theatres and many halls are equipped in advance for such presentations, whereas churches can be awkward, inconvenient and sometimes extremely uncomfortable. You will need to look at the pitfalls as well as the advantages and try to decide how the problems can best be overcome.

WHAT KIND OF A BUILDING?

Churches come in all shapes and sizes, so you would be wise to choose your play to suit the building where you are planning to perform. A medieval abbey with a stone vaulted roof would be a hopeless place for a play with quick-fire dialogue, though it might be ideal for Christopher Fry's *The Boy with the Cart*. A small modern church with raked seating (i.e. seating which is tiered) could be the perfect setting for James Bridie's *Mr Bolfrey* but a spectacular production of John Bunyan's *Pilgrim's Progress* might look a little out of place there.

Before you even begin to choose your play, it would be advisable for your director, designer and stage manager to make a careful check of the proposed church. In all too many traditional buildings you may find that the only available space for the main action of the play is in the narrow gap between the choir stalls, where there is scarcely room for three to stand abreast. It may be impossible to enter the acting area except from stage left, or stage right, or even conceivably from front-of-house. The pulpit, lectern, screen and pillars may all provide obstacles to movement, sight and sound.

So, what do you do? At one extreme, you can build a sort of

theatre inside the church. A deep purse and a reliable carpenter may be able to provide you with a good-sized stage, possibly extending over some of the front pews, with broad steps on either side for entrances. There may be nothing to stop you from erecting a backdrop or even a box set which has scenery at the back and sides of the stage. This uncompromisingly theatrical approach should put almost any kind of production within your scope, but it will have been bought at a price. The disadvantages of pretending you are in a purpose-built hall are twofold: first, the imitation will never be quite as good as a real theatre; second, and rather more seriously, you are throwing away one of your greatest assets – the personality and atmosphere of the church itself.

The opposite extremity is to cut your dramatic coat entirely to your architectural cloth. If there is no room for furniture, then choose a play that can do without it. Where the echo makes speech difficult, depend as far as possible on singing and action or get your cast to speak slowly and oratorically like the old barnstormers. The disadvantages of this policy are too obvious to be worth listing, but you may find that it offers some compensations. Many churches are in their own way highly dramatic venues, with a variety of levels and almost theatrical contrasts of light and shadow. Although scenery and curtains may feel out of place, a church provides a natural background for banners, and there are few backdrops to compare with a really fine altar and reredos. The pulpit can often be used to great dramatic effect. Noah might begin his building of the ark there; angels or demons can appear from its depths and disappear again. Sometimes it is even possible to stage scenes in different parts of the church with the audience following the performers from one place to another.

Most directors will settle on a compromise between these two extremes by trying to offset the worst problems of church performance without spoiling the atmospheric effect of the building. In particular, where the acting area is hopelessly small or too low for the audience to see the action, you may well be able to borrow or construct a temporary stage, while hardly affecting the appearance of the church at all.

One of the difficulties of using such a platform without a curtain is, of course, the lack of space at the sides of the stage. After playing in small theatres or halls, your group will be used to complete invisibility when they are offstage. Now they will need to acquire a new skill which can be termed 'the invisibility technique': characters can leave the platform and remain seen, but totally unnoticed, because they will be frozen into a silent stillness and become, in their imaginations, 'non-people', watching the action but never taking a part in it. Sometimes there will be pillars or chantry chapels to hide behind. Occasionally, a side chapel can be used as a sort of dressing room or green room. But, wherever the actors go, the discipline of silence, as well as stillness, is vital.

One practical point about staging, especially if it has been borrowed, is to make sure your stage manager and carpenter have tested it for safety: try the steps which lead up to it and tread out every bit of the platform itself. Some years ago, when Theatre Roundabout was presenting *Brother Francis* in Ludlow Parish Church, the director was checking the lighting and walked to the far end of a platform four feet six inches high. Suddenly one of the downstage corners tilted under him, and it was only because two members of the cast had the presence of mind to jump on the other end that he was saved from a nasty fall.

Platforms can be awkward in other ways. They can often spoil a dramatic moment by squeaking, groaning or clattering. Test your platform for unwanted noises and, if necessary, plug the squeaking or groaning board. Carpeting is always useful for reducing noise. Where it is not available, ask your cast to wear rubber-soled shoes – unless the sound of footsteps is to be a stage effect, in which case, an ominous 'clack-clack' can send shivers down the spine.

Some churches, especially reasonably modern ones, are well provided with acting areas; but these, though roomy, may not be high enough to make the actors visible to a large audience on the flat. In church services, clergy normally stand when speaking, but characters in plays will need to be seen when sitting or even lying down on the floor. A platform is desirable, simply to give height. If a full stage is impossible, a selection of rostra can at least give a variety of heights and enable those beyond row three to see more than just the heads and shoulders of the actors. In fact, all variation in height is an asset when grouping, and the cast should be encouraged to use any available steps, the pulpit or even chairs and tables in order to break a sense of visual flatness.

NEED TO BE SEEN

While it is vital that your cast should perform at a level where the audience can see them, it is equally important that the play should be properly lit, and in a church this is not always easy. In contrast to a theatre, which is designed to concentrate the audience's attention on the stage, a church has a worrying number of distractions – candles, hymn boards, the pulpit, the lectern, Mothers' Union banners, monumental plaques, Sunday school collages, and so on. The existing lights are often inadequate and may even work against you, illuminating places that you would like to conceal but leaving the actors' faces in darkness. Oddly enough, really modern systems may be even more intractable than the old naked bulbs dangling from twenty feet of flex; all too often you may find that the nave lights are of a new and improved pattern that takes ten minutes to warm-up. You will be very lucky if the church has suitable equipment to light your play adequately.

If not, then it is urgent to inspect the electric supply to discover how much lighting it will support. You will almost certainly need a skilled electrician who can lay a network of carefully secured cables.

In order to light the acting area without drawing attention to all the distractions around it, you would be well advised to use theatre spotlights, which give a bright beam but with a soft and almost imperceptible edge. The ideal angle is between thirty and forty-five degrees above the heads of the actors and about the same angle to either side. If the church has a gallery, it will make an ideal place to put the lights. Otherwise, you may have to mount them on stands, if possible hidden behind a pillar, to which they can be firmly attached, or you may be able to run a two-inch barrel under an arch and hang spotlights from that. Whatever method you use, remember that spotlights have a much more magical effect when they are angled from the side so as to mould everything they light in three dimensions. On the other hand, lighting from straight in front seems to flatten everything out.

If you have no spotlights of your own, you may be able to borrow them from a nearby school or theatre, though you may have to pay a hire charge. Don't be tempted to make do with the so-called spotlights used by photographers or window dressers, which are quite unsuitable for a play. Above all, avoid any form of floodlighting, since it will make the distractions worse than ever.

Coloured lighting can be helpful, but should be used sparingly and as unobtrusively as possible. Many churches point to the east, so normally sunlight comes through the south or stage-left windows. You can subtly reproduce this effect by using straw-coloured filters on stage-left lights and steel-coloured filters on stage-right lights. A more lush version might use old gold and surprise pink. Do make sure that your lighting operator is not visible to the audience, who will be distracted if they can see him or her turning the pages of a script. But the operator must have a clear view of the stage. Sometimes a screen can be helpful, or a large pillar, or the lights can be worked from the back of the church or a gallery.

Costumes are very important and help to concentrate the attention of audiences. Bold, broad outlines define characters. Once again, remember that the church is full of eye-catching colours and patterns, so that there is a need for simplicity. If the play is biblical or historical, you have a great opportunity to create colourful effects. Often the impact of the drama is enhanced by the use of a limited range of colours – say, from warm brown through yellow through orange to flame, or from grey through green through blue to purple.

Some of the most striking effects can be created by the use of black and white only. When Theatre Roundabout presented their two-person version of William Thackeray's *Vanity Fair*, their costume range was from white through grey-green to black. Interestingly enough, when Cheek by Jowl presented the same play many years later, they chose the same limited but striking colour scheme. The use of totally formalised costumes can be surprisingly effective for performances in churches. For the chorus in E. Martin Browne's production of *Murder in the Cathedral,* Stella Mary Pearse designed identical, almost shapeless dresses in a very heavy, beautiful material which looked like medieval tapestry; and when Theatre Roundabout presented Henri Gheon's *The Way of the Cross* in the 1960s, the cast wore identical, long robes in a colour range from cream to dull green and rust to brown. The use of plain, non-fussy costumes was an aid to the effectiveness of grouping where body language became apparent and the expressions of hands and faces were heightened.

It is important for your group to appoint someone to design costumes and scenery. And, of course, you will – if the play is to be biblical or historical – need a good-natured and adaptable wardrobe manager, who may need helpers if the cast is large. It is often advisable to look first for inexpensive and suitable materials, bearing in mind that furnishing materials are usually the most effective, and to plan the colour scheme from what is available.

For modern plays some sense of coordination can achieve telling results and, for this reason, a designer will be needed, if only to prevent the muddled effect that results from each member of your cast deciding for themselves what they should wear. Modern clothes can be used to distinguish characters if thoughtfully planned. A checked shirt or a red blouse can catch the eye, but more than one of each will only confuse the audience. Remember that costumes send out important signals about character. Think of the White Queen in *Through the Looking Glass* with her untidy shawl and her hair dropping out of its bun, while the Red Queen looks as neat as a new pin. Once again, keep to clean lines and simple designs which catch the eye.

This brings us to the question of the performers' faces. Once again, the need is for a clear impact and the use of make-up must, of course, depend on the available lighting. The stronger the lighting, the more the need to emphasise the features, though where it hasn't been possible to get strong lights, or where the performance is part of a church service, it may be best to use no make-up at all.

Scenery, of course, is part of what the audience sees. Here again, in a church, it is helpful to use simple effects. Churches tend to be vivid, solid, intensely real buildings, which make scenery made from canvas look very flimsy by comparison. Try to avoid a box set. Instead, go for a minimalist setting, using real objects which work with, and not against, the architecture of the church. A bookcase, a pedestal holding a vase of flowers, simple tables and chairs which can be moved between scenes, are often more telling than an attempt at elaborate scenery.

Whatever you choose for your play in a church, never allow scene changes to hold up the flow of the play. In many cases the actors themselves can move the furniture as part of the action. Time lost between scenes is like dropped stitches in a piece of knitting; the loss of continuity is extremely damaging and should be avoided wherever possible.

NEED TO BE HEARD

Churches are often difficult places in which to make oneself heard. Before settling on a church for your production (or a production for your church), get some of your company to try out the sound. While one person speaks from the acting area, let the others listen from different parts of the building. Once you have made your decision, it's most helpful if all the actors concerned listen to each other and decide which of them are sufficiently audible. It is impossible to overstress the importance of being heard or the difficulties which need to be overcome.

Medieval churches with stone vaulting can be so full of echo that words get swallowed up. Newly plastered walls in modern churches sometimes produce the same echo effect. Can anything be done about this? Yes, with patience and determination it can. The greatest aid to clarity lies in the use of consonants. Encourage your actors to think of them as frames that support the vowels inside. Echoes pick up and enhance the vowels till they become a kind of blur. Consonants fight the echoes and help the words to stand out.

In our country there is a tendency to let the vowels do all the work by speaking with loose lips. The lips need to be workers. So does the tongue. The Ps and Bs, the Ms, the Vs and the Ws all depend upon the lips. The Ds and Ts, and the Ls are the chief ones for exercising the tongue. Encourage your actors to practise saying these letters over and over as exercises for the lips and tongue. Tongue-twisters like:

- 'Peter Piper picked a peck of pickled pepper'
- 'The jar of butter tottered on the table'
- 'The dandelions dwindled as they dawdled in the dell'

can be fun to work on, and you could encourage your cast to make up some for themselves.

The church you are planning to perform in may have quite a different problem. It may have a wooden roof, excellent carpeting and even curtains, which not only soak up echo but block out the original sound. In that case your group will need to learn how to project their voices. This doesn't mean that they can afford to give their lips and tongues a rest, but they must also learn to use those cavities behind the cheekbones which help to carry the voice forward. A useful exercise is to get your actors to practise humming on a single note till they feel the front of their face vibrate. Then they can gently open their lips to let the sound escape: 'Mmmm . . . aww . . . aah.' After regular practice they will be able to speak much louder without any temptation to shout.

If the acoustics prove too much for your cast, you may need to use microphones. Fortunately many churches nowadays have a permanent sound system, but always make sure you have permission to use it. The ideal system is to have small radio mikes pinned to the clothes of each performer, but they are not very easy to use. Your technician will need to spend a considerable amount of time making sure they are levelled correctly, and the performers must be taught to keep their mouths at roughly the same distance from their microphone. A cheaper, and perhaps safer, method is to range a line of microphones along the front of the acting area, but even those can give a haphazard effect. Above all, you will have to impress on your cast that the microphones are not there to save them trouble; they will have to be equally careful and vigilant, but in a slightly different way.

THE NEEDS OF YOUR AUDIENCE

Besides practical considerations there is another important point to consider when presenting a show in church, and that is the feelings of the congregation. The very intensity of response generated by performing in a church brings its own dangers. Some of the regular worshippers may be antagonistic to the idea of drama at all. Almost all will be highly sensitive about what you play there. Theatre can be a powerful and intimate force; so can religion. By acting in church you are, as it were, doubling the stakes, with much to gain and even more to lose. Drama exists by laying bare the emotions, church is a place where people examine their souls. It is a great compliment to be allowed into the secret places of other people's lives, but remember the words of W. B. Yeats: 'Tread softly because you tread on my dreams.'

Open-air Performances
Tony Jaggers and Alicia Petty

VENUE

The scope for innovation in open-air theatre is enormous and the magic and excitement of creating your own theatre from nothing is well worth the extra effort. Open-air theatre has endless possibilities, including:

- simple street theatre at minimum expense
- creating your own outdoor theatre for the occasion
- a permanent, fully equipped, lavish open-air venue like the Minack cliffside theatre in Cornwall or the open-air theatre at Regent's Park in London

There are plenty of places to choose from: local council parks, stately homes, National Trust properties, anywhere that might have you – even a large private garden. Many landlords will be happy to host your event without charge as it will attract visitors and potential publicity. However, there will be costs in addition to those of a production in a normal theatre that you should take into account, such as electricity and water supplies, toilet provision, security and access. Also consider interference from external noise, such as road traffic, aeroplanes, general public, other events, church bells or chimes and anything else that might disturb an audience. Unfortunately, your ideal location could be wrecked by something as simple as a nearby busy road. You should also consider and agree with the landlord:

Open-air performances: consider interference from external noise.

- access for rehearsals
- time required to prepare the venue for the performances
- number and duration of performances
- insurance arrangements – particularly public liability. If the landlord is a private individual, it may be fair to reimburse him for any extra insurance he has to take out to cover against theft of his property
- payment for electricity used if via the landlord's meter

Once the venue has been agreed, it will be necessary to carefully site the performing space and audience in relation to the setting sun. If you are performing on summer evenings you do not want your actors or audience to be facing the setting sun. The ideal is for the sun to set either to the left or right and just behind the audience, unless, of course, it is shielded by buildings or trees. Wherever possible, make best use of natural features or buildings – there is no point in performing at a stately home if you build your stage in the car park. But you will need to watch for additional background noises; these can vary from the rustling of the trees in the breeze to the sound of a waterfall if you are near a stream. And find out how close you are to a power supply.

There are various access considerations – can your audience find it easily and park nearby? If there is a long walk to the performance space, consider providing transport (this is particularly important for patrons with limited mobility) – we once used a park's tourist train to bring people from the car park and take them to the toilets during the interval. The other important access issue is for any heavy equipment, such as a seating grandstand, lighting equipment, set, etc. Finally, make sure emergency vehicles will still have access once your theatre is built and that your audience is not sitting on top of the fire-hydrant point.

You will need to consider the security of your theatre during the performance and at all other times. Not only do you not want people disturbing your performance, you do not want anyone stealing or damaging your expensive equipment when you are not there. There are security firms who will provide overnight or twenty-four-hour security cover.

You need to create a controlled environment for your audience and actors. You may want to restrict the audience to only those with tickets. It also means working out the position of your lighting and sound control desks, sight lines and offstage areas and finally where the dressing rooms may be.

As well as the usual copyright clearances for the show you will need a public entertainment licence. See pages 132–4 for more details. Also check whether you need permission for any special effects such as fireworks – this is especially important near the coast where you should inform the coastguards.

SEATING THE AUDIENCE

First decide in conjunction with the local authority how many people you can safely fit into your space. Then balance how many people *might* come against how many you *need* to cover your expenses (at a reasonable ticket price). Some hosts may set their own prices – as at the Minack – or may want deliberately accessible prices, such as with a local council park. You now need to consider if you will provide seating, or if people will bring their own seats, or sit on the ground. The latter option is possible in a natural amphitheatre. However, there are drawbacks if you do not provide seating: the audience is harder to control, particularly with sight lines and safety issues, and if the audience is not comfortable the actors may not get their complete attention.

If you provide your own seats remember that every member of the audience needs to have a good view of the stage and so you will probably need to provide raked seating (e.g. rostra) or a grandstand. Seating must conform to the health and safety requirements of the local authority.

Grandstands can be hired in all sorts of different shapes and sizes and although they are the more expensive option they can seat a lot of people in a small area. For example a 366-seat grandstand with twelve rows and thirty seats in each row (six extra in the back row at the top of two aisles) needs about seventeen metres by nine metres.

One advantage of a grandstand is that many of them can be erected over 'obstacles', such as small flower beds, or small 'street furniture', such as bollards; and they can even cope with uneven ground. One of the major considerations is whether or not to have a roof. While a roof protects the audience from the rain it can spoil your production – we had to roll our roof back or half our audience would not have been able to see the balcony scene in *Romeo and Juliet*. And most grandstand roofs will offer a letter-box view of the stage area to those on the back rows. And even if it is called on to protect the audience from the rain, the drumming noise on the roof will quite likely be louder than the actors. You can hire metal or wooden grandstands and you need to choose which serves you best. A metal stand may require earthing (for electricity) – please check with your technicians. Because of their demand at sporting events, you will need to book your stand as early as possible and although many of the big hire companies deal with thousands of seats on a daily basis, most are very helpful and efficient in supplying smaller events. Check how long they will take to set up and dismantle.

Allocated or reserved seats? Presuming that you have a fixed number of seats you will need to decide if you are selling reserved seats as you would in a traditional theatre. The advantage is you can have different prices and you have fewer problems fitting everyone in before the show starts. On the other hand a first come, first served system encourages audiences to arrive early to get a good seat and heightens the general anticipation; however, this may well inhibit a leisurely 'picnic in the park' first. If you want to sell your tickets from more than one box office or outlet, then a reserved seat policy may be difficult to administer.

For a promenade performance it is probably sensible to begin the show in a seated area (unreserved) but thereafter you can offer a mixture of standing or seated viewing.

LIGHTING

There is a magical moment during an evening open-air performance when natural light fades and artificial light takes over. Most audiences will not realise this is happening but will find themselves drawn into an enchanting atmosphere of subtle darkness, very unlike the warm sunshine that began the show. On the other hand you may decide to perform the whole show in daylight in which case you will need to start early enough. However, if you decide to light your show, you will need to think about the following:

- Stage lighting requires electricity! With a big lighting rig you will either need access to a three-phase power supply or to hire a diesel power generator with the necessary noise abatement. If you do hire a generator, consider its location carefully as the low-frequency hum can become a distraction. If you are a long way from the power supply point, the cabling and appropriate equipment can be hired but may be quite expensive.
- However large or small your lighting and sound rig is, it will need to be inspected by a qualified electrician before the first performance. Phase balance, residual current protection, maintained (safety) lighting, water-proofing and tidiness, etc., should be checked. Be prepared to show an inspection report to the local authority.
- A comprehensive lighting rig will need towers and gantries to hang lamps from and while these might be tricky to erect, they are feasible if you have the time, budget and a good backstage crew. As you will be working at heights, you need to pay particular attention to safety; we have found it essential to have a cherry picker to gain access to gantries and lighting towers. (Incidentally, a scaffold tower carrying any weight will require ballast to keep it steady and safe in the wind – we have used sand and guy ropes with ground anchors in the past. Ask a civil engineer to do the necessary calculations.)
- You will also need a control panel, with a good view of the stage and protected from the elements and somewhere to put the lighting dimmer racks.
- Try to route any cables to avoid possible contact with the public. If cable joints are necessary they need to be fully protected from any rain.
- Alternative forms of light can make an open-air production really special. You can consider flaming torches – subject to fire officer approval – or car headlights, or even battery-powered torches. Using light from inside a

building to produce dark shadows outside can be very effective.
- Although not really a source of light, the moon can provide a magical element: at Minack, the moon, when full, rises over the sea directly behind the stage.

Regardless of stage lighting you will need lights for the audience, both safety lighting in case of a power failure and ordinary house lights for the end of the show. You may also need lighting to help people get back to the car park. This could be as simple as the cast with torches, or trees hung with lanterns or festoon lights.

SOUND

In a normal theatre auditorium the sound bounces back off walls and seats to assist with audibility. Not in the open air. Plus the distance between the back of the acting area and the back of the seating may be quite large, so being able to hear your actors, and them being able to hear their cues, becomes a vital part of your production planning. There are a number of things to consider:

- Voice amplification – do not amplify artificially unless you really have to. Rather than see this as a problem, encourage your actors to project their voices (not shout) and speak clearly. If it is essential, then only mike the people who really need it; if you do this you will need a mixing desk to ensure the correct balance between the voices and ensure that the amplification can be turned off when an actor leaves the stage.
- You will need to relay the production to the backstage areas (such as dressing rooms) and, most importantly, to all stage entrances: even if the entrances are quite close, it may be difficult for an actor to hear a cue spoken by another actor on stage facing the audience.
- Communication facilities – walkie-talkie or talkback – to allow the technical staff and front-of-house to liaise are essential. It is sensible to have such facilities at all stage entrances (useful in the event of an emergency) as well as for the stage manager, control box and front-of-house manager. However, make sure that any such communication cannot be heard by the

audience. Also, check that the frequency you are using does not interfere with any other broadcasts.

- Usual facilities for sound effects and incidental music, with waterproof loudspeakers in the auditorium area, may be needed.
- To avoid mains interference, power your sound equipment from a different source than the lights.
- Finally, in case of an emergency, the stage manager and FOH manager should know where the nearest landline telephone is.

REHEARSALS

Hopefully you will be able to rehearse in your space before the theatre is built. This will help the actors get used to working in the open air. Again, this requires some planning:

- Get agreement in advance from your landlord.
- Book it into the rehearsal schedule, so that your group can plan transport.
- In a public area you will attract attention. You can use this to your advantage by giving leaflets to onlookers. But this may put your actors off, so do not expect their best performances.
- If you are using any dangerous equipment – like swords – ensure areas are cordoned off, or guarded, to make sure that the public are protected as much as possible.
- Watch out for children and animals.

An outdoor stage is always very different from the standard indoor version; for a start it will invariably be very much bigger, may have an unusual shape and may involve complex routes to get to the various entrances, balconies, roofs or windows that you may be using. The actors will need to get used to speaking facing the audience and projecting their voices. Also, actions need to be more exaggerated. Some outdoor locations pose particular problems: for example, at Minack the auditorium towers above the stage as it is literally the cliffside. There, the actors need to get used to tilting their heads back and abandon any idea of wearing wide-brimmed hats!

AUDIENCE AMENITIES AND INFORMATION

Catering for the audience's needs is your biggest concern in an open-air setting because you have to create all the amenities you normally take for granted in a traditional indoor theatre. Here are most of the things you will need:

- Sign-posting to the venue – do not presume that all your patrons will know where to go. AA/RAC signs are possible but are quite expensive. You can also make your own road signs by stencilling on to lightweight plastic 'House for Sale'-type boards, but these must be approved by the highway authority. Otherwise, give clear instructions and/or maps. Once away from the public highway, you can put up your own signs to the theatre, the picnic area, toilets, etc., but liaise with the landlord.
- Car parking will need to be provided, preferably at no cost to the patron, even if that means waiving the normal charge – obviously to be agreed in advance with the landlord and then clearly indicated. Provide clear signs on how to get from the car park to the theatre – you may even wish to have someone from your front-of-house team there to greet people, show them where to park and point them in the right direction for the auditorium.
- Patrons with limited mobility need special consideration, particularly in needing to park nearby or to be dropped off close to the auditorium. Again, consider a map of the location. You will need to allocate spaces in the auditorium for wheelchair users and their friends. Remember, it is important to value and not marginalise those with disabilities, so take time and consideration in planning accessibility.
- Public transport may be tricky if you are in an out-of-the-way spot – as most country houses and parks are. However, it is worth researching and publicising information if such transport is available.
- Toilets need to be provided and, something all theatres should be made aware of, women need more toilet stalls than men. If you do not consider this when planning your toilet facilities you will end up with long queues

and an even longer interval. Remember that people with limited mobility (including wheelchair users) may also need access to these facilities. If necessary toilets can be hired. For a 500-seat theatre and a thirty-minute interval you will probably need eight female cubicles, four male cubicles and eight urinals, with an appropriate number being fully accessible. If hiring portable toilets make these as luxurious as you can afford.

- Refreshments may be easily provided if there is already an on-site catering management. However, you may need to consider providing additional refreshments. If you want to sell wine, etc., you will need a liquor licence. Alternatively, you could ask a local pub to provide a bar but the prices will be higher to recover their labour costs. They will need to get a temporary liquor licence. See pages 135–6 for details of the liquor licensing rules. If the weather is grim, it may be good to offer hot drinks – see if this is possible. Even better is to offer some food. We have used external caterers and bars with great success and you may even be able to charge them a franchise fee for the privilege. A nice idea here is to 'theme' the refreshments – for example, Italian food for an Italian-based play. Large plastic boxes or bags labelled 'bottles' and 'waste' will help to keep the place tidy. Any catering facilities must comply with health and safety regulations. More details are on page 157.

- If the venue is suitable you may wish to encourage your patrons to 'picnic in the park' before the show. This helps make it a bigger social occasion and your hosts will be delighted at their park being widely enjoyed.

- As mentioned earlier, you will need to be able to control your auditorium area – ensuring that no one can get in until the 'house' is officially open. However, the foyer-type areas with bar, etc., can be open to the general public.

- Provide first -aid facilities. The easiest way is to invite the local Red Cross or St John's Ambulance Brigade to attend; they do not normally charge, but a donation to their funds is welcome. And remember, your actors or technicians may need them.

- Finally, if your theatre is near water you may need to warn the audience about insects: advise they bring some repellent!

TICKET SALES AND MARKETING

Marketing an outdoor production is no different to a normal indoor performance except that you need to make it clear that it is outdoors. If you are on tour then a company T-shirt or sweatshirt can assist your publicity drive in the area. If it is a holiday area, then you will need a small team to distribute handbills and posters to tourist attractions as well as shops and hotels. A publicity stunt with members of the company in costume handing out leaflets is a good way of showing people that you are 'in town'. If you are building your theatre in a park, make sure that there are posters or leaflets telling the public what the building work is for.

The local theatre may be happy to offer box-office facilities for a commission. The advantage is that they are used to handling tickets and providing accurate accounts. Most now provide their own custom-printed tickets and this will save you the expense of printing your own. If selling via company members you need to keep a very careful log of who has what – and more importantly who has paid. A simple order form can help with this. If you sell via unusual outlets, make it simple and give them very clear instructions – we would not advise using a reserve system in this case. You will need a temporary box office on the night to deal with any door sales or returns.

Any patron with a ticket needs additional information. We give out a small leaflet detailing the essential information they will need to make their evening enjoyable. You may consider putting some of this information on your poster or flyer – such as 'free car parking' or 'barbecue and licensed bar available'.

WEATHER

You cannot plan for this, but you can consider all the possibilities:

- Is the stage area safe to act and work on? It may be waterlogged, or covered in vast puddles.

- Are your electrics safe? Do not take any risks, always check first.
- Will your scenery cope with the wind? Banners and flags can cause appalling damage if they escape, but you can rectify this at the construction stage of large canvases with wind-release vents. Remember wind can also snatch voices away, so consider this with your sound engineer.
- The afternoon summer sun can be very powerful. Advise on hats, sunscreen and drinks – otherwise your first aiders will be working overtime.
- Encourage wet-weather gear and ban umbrellas, since they will obscure the view of people behind. You may consider obtaining plastic ponchos on sale-or-return from a local leisure park (the kind you buy before hurling yourself down the log flume).
- While the early evening may be very warm the temperature will drop quickly once the sun goes down, so jumpers, coats, blankets, etc., are essential, particularly for those with children.

Your wardrobe and props departments will also be anxious about protection of costumes, furniture, props and the set. You need to be particularly careful about borrowed or hired costumes – is there anything in the contract banning their use outdoors or in wet weather? One possible solution is to wear see-through plastic ponchos. You will also need drying facilities for the costumes.

Finally, you need a policy on cancellation in the event of bad weather – but do not panic too much beforehand, we have only lost two performances in the last ten years. You need to have a clearly stated foul-weather policy that is available when the ticket is purchased – include it in your additional information leaflet. A typical policy would be:

- full refund, or tickets for an alternative night, if the performance is cancelled before, or within half an hour of, starting
- no refund if the show has continued beyond half an hour (we always try to go at least to the interval)

Do not offer refunds on the door (you will not have enough cash), give the audience an address to write to, forwarding their tickets. However, if you have enough tickets for future performances you could offer these. The decision to cancel a show lies with the house manager and stage manager, since they are collectively responsible for the safety of the audience and actors.

It is possible to buy pluvious insurance (compensation if it rains), but this can be extremely expensive. An alternative approach to the problem of a cancellation due to weather is to schedule performances for alternate days and then insert an extra performance if necessary.

STREET THEATRE

If you are performing in the street, you will need to inform the local police. Consider:

- some towns and cities have by-laws and you may not be allowed to perform in certain areas
- if you have special requirements regarding movement through one-way streets or pedestrianised areas, always check first
- if you are using swords or fireworks, get permission
- provide safe storage of props/scenery between performances
- consider alternative sites in case of bad weather

Street theatre can be great fun and generally does not require elaborate 'theatre construction'. A 'cart' is the traditional focus for street theatre and this can be used for simple scenery (we constructed Noah's ark on a cart) and storage of props, etc.

THEATRE CONSTRUCTION

If you are building a theatre from scratch, you will need to consider the following:

- Plan the sequence of build – from an empty space, through to a fully equipped theatre.
- Safety is paramount – appoint a health and safety officer if you can or make

sure the stage manager is fully aware of the regulations including hard hats, safety at heights, etc. Also you need a competent qualified electrician.

- It is a good idea to have someone on hand who has a first aid at work qualification during rigging and de-rigging.
- If you are having a grandstand this will dictate where your lights, cables, etc. go. It is best to install this first.
- Next come the lighting towers and gantries (if you are having them) – all electrical gear can then be rigged as required. You need to make sure you have enough time and darkness before opening night to get your lighting design focused and plotted. Midsummer will only offer a few hours of opportunity.
- Do not forget your dressing rooms, toilets, bar, box office, etc. They will need electric power.
- Hiring some equipment will be essential – grandstand, lanterns, etc. – however, you may be able to be creative and borrow some stock items from local businesses in exchange for publicity and complimentary tickets – for example, scaffolding, ballast sand, cherry pickers and security fencing to screen off the auditorium. Many of these could be obtained from builders' suppliers or hire centres.
- When placing contracts, discuss the practicalities of the situation with your supplier: for example, access difficulties such as narrow roads, or low bridges or trees; the sort of ground any construction is to be on; availability of water for toilets etc. Prepare a specification or get the contractor to provide one and agree in writing. Shop around and keep records of whom you have asked and what has been agreed. On-site meetings are often essential for things like the grandstand. Finally, give your supplier a map of how to get there, pointing out the correct access route.
- On a point of general safety make sure you have sufficient (and the right type of) fire extinguishers.
- Remember that many older buildings are listed and you will not be able to make any modifications or add any fixings and you should take extra care not to cause any damage to the fabric of the building.
- Lawns and gardens may need protection. Consider the solidity of the ground for heavy items as well as vehicle access.
- Finally, be especially careful when de-rigging; this is often done on the night immediately after the final performance – get your electrician to rig

some simple floodlights to help you see what you are doing. Also, make sure there are adequate arrangements including access for contractors to pick up any borrowed or hired equipment.

THE SET

As mentioned earlier, wherever possible make best use of natural features or buildings, so we suggest you keep your set to a minimum. Your audience have an imagination and you can create the essence of any scene with just a few appropriate props and furniture. However, there may be specific items that are essential to the plot. Remember that your set needs to be (as far as is possible) securely fastened (but removable if you wish to take it inside each night), weatherproof and fireproof.

BACKSTAGE FACILITIES

You will have to create a backstage area for the actors with:

- dressing rooms – with areas for men and women. If you cannot get a room inside a building, use caravans or a marquee
- toilets
- props areas – for both during and after the show

FRONT-OF-HOUSE

You will need a manager and various staff to:

- sell tickets and handle returns
- check tickets as people enter
- ensure all gaps in the auditorium are filled if not pre-allocating seats – asking people to move up if necessary

- make safety announcements before the performance begins. We would also suggest that the audience be asked not to use flash photography as this can be distracting (and possibly dangerous) to the actors and other members of the audience. Also, remind them to switch off mobile phones
- sell programmes. Audiences are not necessarily regular theatregoers – help them with a brief synopsis, but do not tell them the whole story. If your audience has the potential to be international, then translations of the synopsis are very useful and help them to enjoy the show. If you have the budget, get your programmes sealed with a plastic coating when they are printed. It will stop them going soggy in the rain!

AND FINALLY . . .

These suggestions are to work in parallel with the other areas included in this handbook. We have found working in the open air tremendously exciting and challenging and well worth the extra effort. Memorable occasions include the fairies disappearing into the distance in the wood behind the acting area in *A Midsummer Night's Dream*; Romeo and Juliet being cremated at the end of a production seen in India; Ariel saying his final lines in *The Tempest* from high up a tree; Sir Toby Belch and his cronies in *Twelfth Night* returning from a night on the town in a vintage Rolls-Royce car; and the moon rising behind Juliet's deathbed at Minack. Your ideas and imagination can create a really magical evening at the theatre.

Performing at Festivals
John Scowen

INTRODUCTION

Festival work is a coming together of groups who enjoy drama and enjoy performing shows. Some groups produce shows to enter festivals, while others perform their last show in a festival because it falls around the same time as their run. Whatever you decide to do, enter for the fun of it and you will find lots of other people who also enjoy entering festivals.

ENTERING A FESTIVAL

If your group has never entered a drama festival before, it may be helpful to go along to one before you make a decision, watch how the festival operates and talk to the organisers and the teams that are entering. Many festivals take the form of a competition. Try to go along on more than one night, perhaps at the beginning and the end of the festival, so that you can hear the adjudicator. If you then decide your group would like to take part, then your first step could be to contact the secretary of the National Drama Festival Association (NDFA) who can provide information on festivals throughout the United Kingdom. Entering a festival should be an enjoyable experience, but it is also an opportunity to develop your skills and learn from other groups and the adjudicator. Before entering, be sure that you, your cast and crew are ready to receive the type of public adjudication that may be given. Most adjudicators will give constructive criticism, which you can use to your advantage for another show.

Most festival organisers will send you all the information you require about the theatre and what is required of you. Remember, some theatres are vastly different to what your group has been used to, and you should make sure you know the size of the acting space and what lighting and sound facilities are available to you.

TYPES OF FESTIVAL

There are various types of festivals, the more popular being the one-act and full-length festivals, but there are other types that your group may wish to try. There are themed festivals, festivals of prose and festivals of public speaking. You must be sure that you enter the right festival for your group. Many people are confused by the fact that there appears to be two British Finals each year. This is because there are two independent drama festival organisations in the UK – the National Drama Festival Association (NDFA) and the All England Theatre Festival (AETF) – each of which organises its own competition. The NDFA is an association of forty-six drama festivals who between them organise twenty full-length festivals and thirty-seven one-act festivals. Festivals take place throughout the year, all over the United Kingdom. Each year in July the NDFA organise an 'All Winners' festival where a selection of some of the best plays that have won an NDFA festival during the year are invited to take part. The NDFA 'All Winners' lasts for a week and includes both one-act and full-length plays.

In England, the other festival organisation is the All England Theatre Festival (AETF). There are similar bodies in the other countries (Drama Association of Wales, the Scottish Community Drama Association and the Association of Ulster Drama Festivals). Each of these bodies organises a series of One-Act Drama Festivals in which the winners of preliminary local rounds go on to compete in divisional, area and national finals. Ultimately, the winners of the four national competitions come together to compete in the British One-

Act Finals. If you are entering an AETF First Round Festival, you must let the festival organiser know in advance whether or not you want to go forward to the next round. The AETF publishes a list of all the festivals and the rounds so you know exactly what the dates are and where they are going to be performed.

You can only opt to go forward in the district your group performs. Before you opt to go forward, make sure you and your team know the dates of all the subsequent rounds and that you are all available to take part and, most importantly, that you can afford to do so. There is nothing more frustrating to the festival organiser than to be told that a group wishes to go forward to the next round only to find, when they win, that they have changed their mind. As far as the NDFA All Winners Festival is concerned, you do not have to decide in advance, although it is helpful if your group is prepared to make the decision quickly if you win the preliminary round.

ONE-ACT FESTIVALS

There are more of these than full-length festivals. For a one-act festival you will be allowed some time to carry out a technical rehearsal but this will be different from festival to festival, so make sure you know what time is allotted to you. You must remember that there are several teams competing so please be patient with the organiser. It could be that you all have to do your technical rehearsal on the same day so there may be a tight timetable, which will be strict to ensure that all teams have their chance to compete fairly.

FULL-LENGTH FESTIVALS

Entering a full-length festival is quite different from taking part in a one-act festival, as you will probably have the whole day to set the show and even rehearse, which is important for some groups.

EDINBURGH FRINGE FESTIVAL

This is one of the largest, and most eclectic, arts festivals in the world. It is not a programmed festival, but rather open to anyone who wants to perform. Each year, about 600 different groups travel to Edinburgh to take part. The festival is organised by the Festival Fringe Society, which produces a yearly guide and definitive festival programme. They provide lists of venues, press contacts and suppliers. Competition for the best venues at the best times is fierce, with approximately 1,500 different fringe shows fighting for good audiences. Register your interest early, and (upon payment of a fee – £12 for 2001) the Fringe Office will send you details. On top of venue hire fees, the Fringe Office will charge commission on all tickets sold by the Fringe Box Office and a fee to appear in the Fringe Programme.

PICKING THE RIGHT SHOW

Many people say that you should ensure you pick the right show for a festival. However, it is more important to pick a show that suits your group and your cast. Adjudicators are there to see what you make of the show you are performing, not to judge your show selection. The disadvantage of picking what might be called a 'worthy' show is that your actors may not be suitable or may not want to take part. You may decide that you should pick a show that would stretch your actors and give them something to get their teeth into; you may choose to pick something that is quite controversial or thought-provoking to challenge both your audience and adjudicator, or you may want to put on something that you would not or could not possibly put on locally because you would not get an audience.

Some festivals have a maximum running time for each show so ensure that you know what this is. If you run overtime points may be deducted and if you cut dialogue you must have the author's permission to do so beforehand. There may be no time limits for the length of the show but be careful not to put on a show that is too long.

LIGHTING AND STAGING

Don't be over ambitious about your lighting, as you will probably only be allowed a standard lighting rig and occasionally one or two special lights that will not affect the rest of the evening. On most nights of a one-act festival there will be two to three shows, so festivals provide the standard rig. This is not to say you cannot have what you want; it is just that they will not be able to move lights around during the intervals. Some festivals will allot a coordinator to look after you, so make full use of their knowledge, it may help to use the time available to your best advantage. For one-act shows, ten minutes may be allowed to set the stage, which will be timed by the festival's nominated timekeeper. Setting the stage means all scenery, furniture, stage props, but not adding lighting effects. At the end of the performance, five minutes may be allowed to strike the set. This may sound a short time, but it is amazing how much can be achieved with thoughtful design and careful preparation.

A good tip is to allot jobs to the crew so that they are not all running around trying to take off the same item. Have one person who is in charge of giving an 'all clear' so that they alone declare when the stage is clear. Although an interesting set can enhance a performance, it is easy to be over ambitious. However, remember that just because you are entering a festival you do not have to restrict yourself to one chair and the use of black drapes. If you are flexible in what you do, you will find that the experience will be more enjoyable and the group won't be on tenterhooks or stressed about what they are doing. Please note that all props and set must be brought on the day and removed after the performance.

Some festivals will build and supply your set for you, so if you are entering make sure you know this. Some theatres have safety curtains that come down during the interval; in these cases, do not have your set across the front tabs. The stage manager will not allow this and you may find your acting space further restricted.

Remember to ensure you have permission for all special effects that you want to use. Do not turn up with pyrotechnics (including smoke) unannounced.

ADJUDICATIONS

Some people dread them, some people love them. One of the features of entering a festival is for an adjudicator to look at your work and give you constructive criticism about how you went about it. You do not have to agree with the adjudicator; you do not have to take on board what is said, but what you should do is look upon the adjudication as an experience and keep an open mind. There should be an opportunity after the adjudication to meet with the adjudicator and talk about the show in greater detail. This will give the adjudicator a chance to explain the assessment, and a chance for you to put your views forward. Listen to what is being said and make notes to disseminate to the cast afterwards. But whatever you do, do not go away from a festival feeling upset. A good adjudicator will always have something positive to say about your show! You can also obtain a written adjudication of your show, from which you can learn so much and that will help you if you intend to enter again. It is a good way of helping the actors to work on their technique and how to look at shows in a different way. There is a cost for a written adjudication so make sure you budget for it.

PITFALLS

There are many pitfalls that you may encounter when entering a festival and you should ensure that you are aware of as many as possible so that your performance is a polished and enjoyable experience. Remember to get confirmation that your entry has been received and that the night you perform is confirmed as part of the programme. Contact the festival organiser to ensure they have not mislaid any of your details. Ensure you give the festival organiser the correct information in plenty of time to produce the publicity for the festival. Make sure your cast is available and willing to travel. If at the last minute a member of your cast decides to pull out, can you replace them?

It is sometimes a good idea to visit the theatre beforehand with other members of the cast so that a few of you know the way. Make sure you have adequate parking and that you can offload your scenery.

Make sure your have the right to perform, so get copyright clearance early. Photocopied scripts are not acceptable, unless specific permission has been granted. Make sure you have contacted the publishers and they have granted permission in writing. Festival organisers will not just take your word for it. Any cuts that you want to make to the script must have been agreed with the copyright owner. For more details see pages 83-97.

Make sure you read the rules and regulations carefully: many festivals have different rules, mainly because of the way in which the venue is run, so do not assume that because you have entered one festival it will be the same for the next.

COSTS

Always make sure you have budgeted for the festival show. It is very disappointing to the cast if you are all enthusiastic only to find that you cannot go to the festival because the budget will not allow it. Carefully consider all transport costs, which typically form a large part of a budget for a festival performance. It may be possible to take smaller items in someone's car which could cut down the hire fee costs. You could plan some fund-raising beforehand to boost the budget or apply for a National Lottery grant. Try anything, but be sure you can afford to produce the show before your group completes the application process.

NATIONAL LOTTERY BIDS

Lottery bids are something that most groups forget about when entering a festival while other groups apply for Lottery bids to perform in festivals again and again. Applying for a Lottery bid is a very good idea especially if it is your first time, but make sure your bid is robust enough. Ensure that you put all the details down that are needed, and ask your group members to participate and look over what is written before you submit the bid. Take into account everything that you will need, because once you have submitted your application, you will not be able to change it. If your local authority has a Lottery officer, discuss the bid through with them to ensure you have filled in the forms correctly and your group can meet any funding criteria. You may also want to contact your arts board who will have information on how to make a bid for Lottery money.

CONCLUSION

If your group is ready and willing to perform a show in a festival, and has made proper preparation, all participants will have a wonderful time. It will give members of your group the chance to learn and share expertise, and there is much to be gained from meeting the challenges of unfamiliar stages, auditoria, equipment, facilities and new audiences.

2　The Show

The Budget

Managing a group's money may seem rather dull compared to performing in a show. But without sufficient cash resources, the show cannot take place. A budget is a simple tool, which can help monitor this precious resource.

As well as a general picture of your group's financial health, the show's organisers should have a particular interest in the costs and expenses relating to each show. With someone responsible for each element of the production, your group should try to prepare and stick to a budget. Allotting some time to budgeting in the early part of the planning process will make sure that the group can decide whether or not it has sufficient resources to produce a particular show.

Most costs that a group incurs during any particular year will relate to its productions. However, the group may have some running costs that it incurs regardless of whether it mounts a show. These costs could include sending letters to its membership, hiring rooms for committee meetings or insurance charges. Similarly, the group's main income generator may be the sale of tickets to members of the audience, but other income may be generated by membership fees or fund-raising. It is therefore important not to discuss a budget in isolation, but rather as part of the larger picture of your group's finances.

EXAMPLE BUDGET

A typical budget for a show might be:

PROJECTED INCOME	£	£ Total
Ticket sales (full price)	30,000	
Ticket sales (concessions)	10,000	
Programmes	2,000	
Sponsorship & Advertising	1,000	
Refreshments	1,000	
TOTAL INCOME		45,000
LESS PROJECTED OUTGOINGS		
Hire of Venue	12,000	
Royalties	10,000	
Hire of Scripts / Band Parts	500	
Band expenses	4,000	
Lighting	3,000	
Sound	2,000	
Set	4,000	
Props	1,000	
Costume	3,000	
Make-up	500	
Marketing	2,000	
Programmes & Ticket printing	1,000	
Refreshments & Hospitality	500	
TOTAL OUTGOINGS		43,500
PROJECTED SURPLUS (DEFICIT)		1,500

This example is not exhaustive. Each show in each venue will have its own particular costs. Be realistic when setting a budget. If you cannot be sure that you will sell all tickets at full price, do not budget for 100% full houses for each performance.

The first budget will always be the hardest to prepare, because of the risk that some expenses were not planned. There will also be a strong temptation to base a budget on records relating to previous shows. Only do this after the group has reviewed a full breakdown of the actual income and expenditure of the production (rather than the projected figures, which might have been incorrect). Also check that there are no fundamental differences between the two shows – as a rule of thumb, the larger the cast, the bigger the budget. It is likely that some elements of the budget will need to change – if nothing else, due to the effects of inflation.

Once a budget has been drawn up, the group should decide what to do with it. This may not be as simple as it sounds. Someone should be responsible for each part of the expenditure shown on the budget. That person should be aware of the constraints of the budget, and the effect of overspending. Timetable regular meetings during rehearsals to review actual income and expenditure against the projected income and expenditure. It may be possible to adjust the budget to avoid a financial disaster. However, this flexibility should not be seen as permission for any particular person to overspend.

CASH FLOW

Your group might be in the fortunate position of having some cash in a bank or building society account. Your group should plan to have a float to pay for the expenses as they occur. If your group does not have large resources, it will be important to plan when each major item of expenditure will be incurred. It is likely that some of the larger costs of putting on a show will be payable well before the first performance date. If necessary, negotiate before making any commitments. A venue may be happy to take a small deposit to secure a booking, with the balance of the hire fee payable nearer the date of the show. Other sources of income are highlighted in the Fund-raising section on pages 240–9. See the Liability section for who is ultimately responsible for paying the bills if the group has insufficient funds.

The Production Team

Not everyone who is interested in the theatre wants to have a starring role. Some people are happy with smaller parts, and others prefer not to be on stage at all. A good production will combine the flair of the actors with the 'hidden' talents of the backstage crew. There is no correct ratio of the number of backstage helpers to actors. If it works for your group, it must be correct. The titles given to these jobs are flexible. Some are universally used, but may sound a bit old-fashioned, and some are just local convention.

Most groups have more volunteers for acting roles than there are parts to go round. You might decide to encourage the members who are not acting in the current production to help backstage. Even making tea during rehearsal breaks can provide a social activity for some members, the results of which may be greatly appreciated by the cast. By way of contrast, next time you go to the theatre, check the back of the programme to see the number of people involved in a professional show.

In 2000, not including cast or musicians, *The Lion King* at the Lyceum Theatre in London's West End involved 73 people working for Walt Disney and 141 individuals or companies working for the theatre.

MEMBERS OF THE PRODUCTION TEAM

Some of these tasks are specific to larger scale productions, but the majority are relevant to all shows. Remember that one role can be

Even making the tea may be greatly appreciated by the cast.

split between many people, or one person can take on more than one task, but there should be no doubt who is in charge of a particular area of responsibility. Your group should be clear which decisions are delegated to each member of the production team, whatever their title or role. Also be clear how much feedback the group requires, so that there are no nasty surprises at the dress rehearsal. Consider writing the equivalent of a simple 'job' description for each member of the team, to help create a good structure for communication. This may also help each individual to say 'no' to a special responsibility. It is better to spread these responsibilities as early as possible, especially because a tired member of the team may unintentionally make mistakes that could cost the group or cause injury to others.

Director: This person will be given overall responsibility for bringing together all the elements of the performance. Some groups use the term 'Producer' instead. A 'Producer', especially in the professional theatre, tends to be the person who finds the resources to fund a particular show, and may be involved in hiring the venue, the director and the other members of the management team. A director is someone with an overall view of the show who can shape the production. It is the director's task to bring a script to life, to stage the show and to respond to the skills and technical expertise available within the group. But a director combines an artistic role with a management role. The director must be able to share his or her ideas with the cast and crew enthusiastically and effectively. Therefore the director will often have a background in acting as well as the technical aspects of the performance. The final word usually lies with the director, from casting decisions to the number of curtain calls. It is therefore important that a group can respect the director's work.

Music Director: If a show contains a large amount of music, it is normal for the director to work with a music director, or MD. The MD will work with the cast and the musicians, and is often in charge of the early singing rehearsals. The MD will make sure that the actors know the music well, and are able to sing it to the best of their ability.

Choreographer: A group may use a choreographer to direct the dance routines in a show. A choreographer may also have responsibility for the movement on stage during any large ensemble scenes.

Stage Manager: This is the title for the person in charge of the stage area during a show. The stage manager makes sure that the right scenery and props are on stage at the right time. He or she will be responsible for the safety of the backstage crew and actors on stage. The stage manager may help construct the scenery, and may help shift it during the performance. A stage manager will discuss the director's ideas for the set, and will raise any practical problems as early as possible. The 'get-in' (transporting the scenery to the venue) and the 'fit-up' (putting the scenery in the right place on the stage) will be supervised by the stage manager. If the venue uses painted back-cloths, or suspends scenery from a flying tower, the stage manager may supervise the flying, or may delegate.

Deputy Stage Manager: If the stage manager has a lot to do during a performance, a deputy stage manager (DSM) will 'run the corner'. This means the DSM is in charge of starting, stopping and running the performance. The DSM will follow the script, often from the side of the stage, just out of sight of the audience, and will watch what is going on during the performance to warn the cast when an entrance cue is approaching. At the same time, the DSM will liaise with the other backstage crew, the front-of-house manager and MD. In simpler shows, the DSM may take the role of prompt only.

Property Manager: This is the person in charge of dressing the set with props, and making sure the actors have any props they may need with them at the right time. A props manager may have special responsibility for any unusual items, including guns.

Assistant Stage Managers: If the stage manager, DSM or property manager requires help, assistant stage managers (ASMs) provide an extra pair of hands to help move scenery or operate the house tabs (curtains). ASMs may also have small acting roles or walk-on parts.

Designer: The set may be simple, and designed by the director. If it is more complicated, the task may be taken on by a specialist set designer. The designer may produce plans and supervise the building of the set. Even if the set is being hired, it is likely that adjustments will be required, and a set designer will require some assistance in set construction from carpenters and painters. A designer may also have overall responsibility for the visual aspect of the production, including costumes and make-up.

Lighting Designer: Using stage lighting is often a specialist job. A mood or atmosphere can be created with some clever lighting. A range of lights (also called lanterns or luminaires) are often used, some of which can create special effects. A lighting designer positions and focuses the lights during a technical rehearsal, and may control the lighting during the show. However, s/he may need assistants, especially if follow spots are used.

Sound Engineer: There are two elements to the sound used in a production: the microphones on stage to help amplify the actors' voices, and the live or recorded sounds for music or special effects. Both elements need careful planning and a sympathetic operator for each performance.

Chief Electrician: Larger venues have at least one full-time electrician (LX) for the lighting operator, sound operator or stage manager to consult if they are in any doubt. Because electricity is so dangerous, you may be required by the venue owner or local authority to have a suitably qualified electrician present at the venue during all performances.

Wardrobe Manager: The wardrobe manager will liaise with the director and designer in making, borrowing or hiring the costumes for the production. This person is also in charge of the storing, cleaning and maintenance of costumes during the show.

Make-up Supervisor: Make-up for the stage is very different to everyday make-up. Stage lights can make an actor's face look pale and flat, especially if the audience is sitting some distance away from the stage. Wigs and make-up can also be a specialist job, especially when an actor requires 'character' make-up to emphasise a part of their face.

Marketing Manager: A good marketing manager will plan posters, flyers and other marketing activities to try to sell as many tickets as possible for the show. A marketing manager may also be in charge of ticket printing and programmes, working with the director and designer to make sure the artwork for the publicity material is appropriate to the production. Marketing managers can never have enough helpers!

Box-Office Manager: Unless all ticket sales are handled by the venue owner, someone within the group will need to be responsible for selling tickets and banking the proceeds.

Front-of-House Manager: Lastly, someone should be in charge of the facilities for the audience, both in the foyer and in the auditorium. The front-of-house manager will make sure that a visit to the venue is a safe and enjoyable experience by working with a team of attendants.

FINDING VOLUNTEERS

The best way of finding sufficient volunteers to produce a show is by word of mouth. Even if your group is small, members will probably know other people who are interested in the theatre. Family members of current members are good sources of occasional help. If you need particular skills, it may be worth approaching other groups to see if they know of anyone with that skill. If necessary, create some publicity by announcing your quest to the local community. Backstage help might be a useful way of introducing newcomers to the group, especially if the new volunteers are inexperienced and would like to see how things work during their first show. New recruits may want to get to know the people in a group before committing themselves to a full rehearsal schedule and the stress of a production. Offering a backstage role may be a useful learning process, which could lead to a committed member. However, be flexible. Some groups have 'traditions' that newcomers must work their way up the ranks before they are allowed to audition for a leading role. This may be a useful tool to weed out those members who are less than 100% committed, but conversely, it may put off someone from staying with your group. Remember, you may be competing against other groups or leisure activities, and an enthusiastic volunteer may be disheartened by too rigid a hierarchy. See pages 138–48 for some ideas for different types of marketing.

USING PROFESSIONALS

Sometimes, your group may need to 'hire in' experts. It may be that your group does not have the necessary skills for a particular project, or is short of volunteers. One way of filling this void is to reach an agreement with a professional practitioner. Some may be willing to provide a particular service to the group for no fee, as long as the group agrees to meet any reasonable expenses that the professional incurs. Others may request a fee in return for their input. Before your group commits to engage a professional, be clear on what you expect from the professional in return for their fee. If necessary, agree the scope and timetable for their input, to make sure that time is not wasted in duplicating any work, or gaps left which might require filling at short notice.

Even though these professional relationships are likely to be short, it is important (not only for tax reasons) to distinguish between the professionals who are employed by the group and those who provide services to the group as independent contractors. The first group (employees) are granted statutory rights which must be observed by their employers. These rights include:

- protection from discrimination on grounds of sex, race or (for employers with fifteen or more staff) disability
- maternity leave
- itemised pay statements
- maximum working hours
- minimum wage regulations
- time off work for union and public duties and antenatal care
- (after a qualifying period) paid holiday leave, sick pay, parental leave, a written statement of terms and conditions, notice of termination of employment, redundancy pay.

Although self-employed people do not receive these benefits, some rules (including health and safety legislation) will apply equally to them. Trying to avoid a group's responsibilities by pretending that a relationship is not one of employer/employee by giving a misleading name or false terms and conditions will not succeed, since employment tribunals will look behind any title given to the relationship by the group. The test to decide whether a person is an employee or a self-employed person is complex. However the tribunals are clear that it does not matter whether the individual is paid on a part-time or full-time basis – part-timers have the same employment rights as full-timers.

Some guidance is available from your group's local tax office, but if in doubt take legal advice. See the music section on pages 113-15 for details of hiring professional musicians, and the tax section on pages 258-60 for rules relating to the pay as you earn income tax scheme (PAYE) and national insurance contributions.

The Script and the Rules of Copyright

INTRODUCTION

A great deal of time and effort goes into writing a show. For some people, writing a play or musical is their way of making a living. If so, they receive payment for their work by charging for copies of the script or music, and levying a licence fee in return for granting permission to perform the show. Controlling the terms on which copies may be made, or performances given, are two of the rights ('copyrights') granted to an author of an original 'literary, dramatic, musical or artistic work' by the Copyright Designs and Patents Act, 1988 (the 'Act' for the rest of this section).

Books, scripts, diaries and letters are literary works, and can be protected by copyright if the provisions of the Act are fulfilled. 'Musical works' include symphonies, film soundtracks, even simple advertising jingles. 'Artistic works' include paintings, drawings, photographs and sculptures. Copyright also exists for sound recordings, films and broadcasts.

If your group breaches one of the rights granted to an author by the Act, the author can take legal action to stop the breach and claim a cash sum to cover losses.

WHAT IS PROTECTED BY COPYRIGHT?

A work will be protected by copyright if it is original (i.e. not a copy of an existing work) and if it has been recorded in a permanent form. An original handwritten script may attract copyright protection. An improvised production would only be protected if it is recorded (perhaps in writing or on tape). A make-up design could be viewed as an artistic work, and if photographed, could fall within the provisions of the Act. Similarly, a choreographer's work, once recorded on video, would be protected.

There is no formal registration process which needs to be followed. Copyright is automatic as soon as the work is recorded in a permanent form. The '©' is useful to remind people of the existence of a copyright, but the right remains even if the symbol is not used.

A show may therefore consist of several different elements, each protected by a completely separate copyright, any of which could be owned or controlled by different people. A musical might be based on an existing play, and a play might be based on an existing book. This means that the author of the original source material will own the copyright in the book, but the script for the show, the lyrics and the melodies will each also be protected in their own right. If any element is later recorded, that recording will also attract its own copyright protection.

> *Oklahoma!* is based on the play *Green Grow the Lilacs* by Lynn Riggs, who granted permission to Richard Rodgers and Oscar Hammerstein II to adapt the play into a musical. The Rodgers and Hammerstein Organisation (who now control the copyright in the musical) recently granted permission to the Royal National Theatre to produce a revival of the musical. Both organisations then gave permission for the show to be adapted for a film version which was released in 2000.

Some composers grant permission to other musicians to write an orchestration or other version of their melodies. The orchestrator will own copyright in his or her arrangements of the music, in addition to the original composer, who will continue to own copyright in the melody.

Other members of the creative team might also have their work protected by copyright: the set, costume and make-up designers' drawings or models could be protected as artistic works, and a sound engineer's recording of a special effect could be a protected recording. The graphics and text which make up a poster design for the show could also qualify for protection, either under copyright law, or by other intellectual property rights granted by the Act.

Copyright is a property right, which means that the owner can sell, transfer or grant a licence to another person or body in much the same way as an owner of land can sell or lease his or her property. Where land is sometimes referred to as 'real' property, copyrights (and other similar rights) are sometimes called 'intellectual property' rights.

WHAT IS NOT PROTECTED BY COPYRIGHT?

A title to a play will not normally be protected by copyright. For example, there is more than one play entitled *Phantom of the Opera*. However, if the title is printed using a special typeface or logo, then the typeface or logo may attract copyright protection. A logo could also be protected by a trademark application. Trademarks are distinctive symbols, which, when registered, allow the owner exclusively to control the use of the trademark. This means, for example, only the trademark owner can authorise its reproduction on T-shirts, or other merchandise.

If a title to a show is chosen because it is the same or similar to the name of an existing show, so that the public will book tickets thinking that they are going to see the original, then this can give rise to another legal claim known as 'passing off'. Such underhand methods of gaining an audience can cause lasting damage to the original author, so the courts are prepared to grant that person the right to take steps to stop an infringing use of a name, and the right to recoup lost profits from the diverted ticket sales. See pages 235-6 for other possible consequences of passing off.

Copyright does not exist in the idea of a show. Anyone can write a pantomime based on the idea of a young lad and his magic beanstalk. However, once a play has been written based on that idea, the play will be protected by copyright, and therefore cannot be copied without permission. Any group can write its own version of *Jack and the Beanstalk*, but it would be a breach of copyright if it was an unauthorised copy of John Morley's version of the pantomime.

Copyright only lasts for a period defined by the Act. Once a copyright has expired, the work is no longer protected, and can be freely copied or performed.

DURATION OF COPYRIGHT

In order to bring the United Kingdom's legislation into line with other European countries, the period of copyright was extended in 1996. Before 1996, the period of copyright protection expired fifty years from the end of the year in which the author died. Since 1996, the term has been extended to seventy years. For work created jointly, the seventy-year span starts from the end of the year in which the last of the authors dies. This change in 1996 created some anomalies. Some copyrights had expired under the fifty-year rule, only to be brought back into copyright. This means that the works of George Bernard Shaw, which were due to be copyright-free after 2000, will now be protected until 2020. Perhaps even more confusingly, the copyright in Kenneth Grahame's works have been revived under the seventy-year rule until 2002. Between 1982 (the date his copyright expired) and 1996 many people wrote their own versions of *The Wind in the Willows*, including Alan Bennett. Under the rules of revived (or extended) copyrights, any group may, until 31 December 2002, write their own adaptation of this book, but must agree a fee with Grahame's representatives. After 31 December 2002, the work will be again in the public domain, and no permission or royalty will be payable to Grahame's estate. Remember that Alan Bennett's adaptation has its own copyright, separate from the copyright in Grahame's original book.

Even this fairly complicated position is not without its exceptions. Under the current legislation, copyright in J. M. Barrie's *Peter Pan* will never expire! All royalties for this show are payable to Great

Ormond Street Hospital, and Parliament decided that royalties should continue indefinitely.

Copyright in sound recordings expires fifty years after the end of the year in which it was made or released. Film copyright expires seventy years after the end of the year in which the last surviving principal director, screenplay author, dialogue author or composer dies.

SEEKING PERMISSION

The original author or creator of the work is normally its first owner, and therefore controls whether or not permission should be granted. Most authors do not deal directly with the day-to-day administration of their own copyrights. It is more efficient for authors to ask an agent to deal with the commercial exploitation of their work. It is typical for an author to grant permission to one agent to licence live performances of the work and another agent to deal with licences to film the work. It will be necessary to track down the person who deals with the copyright of a work if your group wishes to:

- copy the work
- issue copies to the public
- rent or lend copies to the public
- perform the work in public (including public readings)
- broadcast the work
- adapt the work

unless one of the statutory exemptions apply. These include:

- private study or research
- criticism or review
- educational use (so plays performed during normal school activities during school time to pupils and teachers do not require copyright clearance)
- use by libraries and archives

All of the exemptions are complex, and your group should seek legal advice if it wishes to rely on them. It may also be necessary to complete some detective work to make sure that you are dealing with the person or organisation who has control of the copyright. A well-meaning author could consent to the use of a copyright-protected work, but it may be that the author has already transferred or assigned the right to control the copyright work to a publisher, agent or film studio. Consider asking for a written promise from the person granting permission that s/he has the right to do so.

CHOOSING AN EXISTING SHOW

Many agents print catalogues of the authors that they represent, which include a list of the names of the plays, musicals and pantomimes; the length of the work; the number of characters in the show and the complexity of the staging required. These catalogues can give your group a very good indication of whether it has sufficient resources to perform a particular work.

Most libraries have a drama section, which includes multiple copies of plays. Otherwise, some publishers are willing to hire out copies of scripts and scores for a group to evaluate. Remember that photocopying of works protected by copyright is prohibited under the Act. If a particular play is out of print, approach the publisher who may be willing for a very reasonable fee to grant the group permission to make copies legitimately.

Once your group has chosen a show, approach the author's agent for permission to perform it. If in doubt, published plays include a note of the name of the relevant agent on the copyright page of the script. If still in doubt, contact a local library, or search on the Internet for details. Names of some of the larger publishers and agents appear in the reference section at the end of this handbook. It is important to obtain permission to perform the show as soon as possible, and in any event before rehearsals start, because granting permission is not automatic. It is common practice for the amateur rights for a show to be withdrawn for a period of time if a professional production is also taking place in the area. The author or agent will also know if other amateur groups have been granted permission to perform the show, and this may be helpful to avoid unnecessary competition for an audience.

The author or agent will require some information in order to draw up a formal licence (or permission) to perform the show. A licence may take the form of a letter or an agreement, but should always be in writing. A typical licence will include:

- the name of the agent
- the name of the group
- the date on which the licence was granted
- the title of the show
- the dates and times of the permitted performances
- the cost of the licence (either as a fixed fee or as a percentage of the box-office receipts). Check whether the fee includes VAT
- any deposit required
- the requirements for providing information relating to ticket sales and the date for final payment of the fee
- supply of scripts or other rehearsal material
- any controls on the wording on tickets, posters or other advertising material

Expect to pay between 7% and 15% of gross box-office receipts as a royalty fee for the larger scale musicals. Some smaller venues and educational establishments may qualify for reduced licence fees – it is always worth asking! Beware when calculating gross box-office receipts, because the agreement may make some assumptions. A lengthy, but not untypical clause might read:

The Group shall pay to the Author for each performance the minimum fee of £100 or 10% of the Gross Box-Office Receipts (whichever is the greater) PROVIDED THAT any tickets issued in return for sponsorship or a donation or given as a free ticket to honorary members of the Group or following the payment of a season subscription shall be treated as having been sold at full price, so that the face value of such tickets shall be included in the Gross

Box-Office Receipts AND FURTHER PROVIDED THAT the
Author reserves the right to charge VAT at the then current rate in
addition to the royalty fee above.

Always read the terms of the licence and keep a copy for the group's
records. The venue owner or festival organiser may wish to see the
licence because the venue may also breach the copyright rules if it
allows a show to be performed without the appropriate consent.
Anyone who permits a public performance to go ahead knowing or
with reason to believe that it infringes copyright in a work is guilty
of a criminal offence. Never think that your group can get away with
not obtaining permission. Remember that the copyright owner
can enforce his or her rights by forcing a group to cancel a show,
and/or by obtaining a court order for payment of a cash sum. The
agents check regularly, and once a reputation has been tarnished,
a group will find it hard to obtain permission from any of
the agents. Insurance policies will not cover any loss suffered by
the cancellation of a show because of the lack of copyright
clearance, since it is a situation which could have been avoided by
the group.

COMMISSIONING A NEW WORK

There will be times when your group will prefer to use specially
created material, rather than anything that already exists. This could
be a specially written script or music, a recording of a sound effect, or
a set or poster design. A member of your group could create the
required material, but it may be necessary to ask a professional to
create the work.

The general rule is that the author of the work (that is, the person
who created the work) will be the owner of the copyright in it. As
always, this rule has a number of special exceptions. The author of a
sound recording is the producer; the author of a film is the producer
and director jointly. If a work is created by an employee in the course

of his or her employment, copyright in the work will belong to the employer unless there is an agreement to the contrary.

Working with a writer can bring a new vibrancy to a project, especially if one of the aims of the project is to involve as large a number of the local community as possible. It also means that the work can be tailored specifically to address a particular local concern, or the particular strengths of your group.

As noted above, the basic rule is that the person who creates the work will own copyright in it. If, for example, your group asks a designer to create an image for the poster for your show, the designer will normally retain copyright in the image. It can be argued that the designer gives the group implied permission to use the image for posters, but it may be more difficult to show that this implied consent includes copying the design on programmes, or on the group's web site, or on publicity T-shirts. If the designer had known about these other uses, s/he may have agreed a different fee for their work. To avoid any grey areas, make the arrangement with the designer clear and record it in writing – dealing in copyrights is one of the few transactions which may be invalid if the transaction is not recorded in writing. The agreement could transfer ownership of the design to the group ('assignment') or may grant the appropriate permissions to use the image ('licence'). Check whether:

- the use of the specially created work is restricted
- the licence only lasts for a limited time
- your group can grant permission to other people to use the work
- your group can transfer ownership of the work

Ownership of the material on which a work has been created does not necessarily confer ownership of copyright. A letter writer will normally retain copyright in its contents although the paper on which the letter is written will be owned by the recipient.

The author's involvement with the newly created work does not end when it is handed over to your group. An author's reputation may be at stake, and it is likely therefore that the author will wish to have some involvement with how the group will use the work. Some authors continue to be involved with the script throughout the rehearsal process. In addition to any agreed level of involvement, the creators of literary, dramatic, musical and artistic works (including films) have moral rights that are enshrined in the Act. The author has the right to be identified as the creator of the work, and the right to veto any distortion of the work which would prejudice his or her reputation. The Writers' Guild of Great Britain and the Scottish Playwrights Society set down minimum fees for their members. Both bodies produce standard contracts which may be helpful.

WRITING A NEW SHOW

There is nothing to stop your group writing your own show, as long as it is original. If your group wants to use existing material as part of the show, permission will normally be required if that material is protected by copyright. Make sure that the people creating the show are aware of the regulations set out above, and agree with them in writing who will own the resulting copyright.

A new work may create some publicity for the group, and if the work is good enough, others may wish to use the material. Consider approaching publishers to see if the play can be commercially marketed – royalty payments would help boost the group's funds. All newly produced scripts must be lodged at the British Library.

ADAPTATIONS

Adapting an existing work is one of the controlled activities covered by the Act. If the original work is protected by copyright, it will be necessary to approach the author (or authorised agent) for permission to create an adaptation. This would include:

- creating a script based on a novel or diary
- creating a musical based on a play

It is likely that the author will wish to have some involvement.

- translations
- arrangements or transcriptions of musical works

If the original work is protected under the revived copyright rules, then permission to make an adaptation is not needed, as long as the author is advised of the adaptation, and royalties agreed.

Your group should take particular care if it wishes to perform a show based on its experience of a film version. Sometimes, in adapting the show for the big screen, the script is changed or new songs added. It may be that the film producers retain copyright in these additions. Check to see that the licence on offer grants permission to produce the show that you think you are producing. If not, your group may need to approach the original author (or agent) for permission to alter the original material, and the film production company (or agent) for permission to use the new material.

SCRIPT CHANGES

It is often very tempting to make some changes to an existing work – it may be your director's opinion that the show would be better if it was shorter, or that certain characters had more to do, or if the whole show was more up to date. However, these types of changes would fall foul of the Act, since they may be regarded as adaptations of the original work. The author may also feel that the changes amount to derogatory treatment of the original work, and could object on the grounds that his or her moral rights have been infringed. Lastly, the licence granted to perform the show may contain a clause which states: 'no alterations or additions are allowed to the script or the music unless the prior permission of the agent is obtained in writing'.

If your group has entered into an agreement which contains the clause above, and subsequently makes alterations to the script, the group could be found to be in breach of the Act, and also in breach of the licence agreement.

A production of *Side by Side by Sondheim* . . . was abruptly closed on March 30 by the show's licensing agent after learning the [theatre's] creative team had made major and unsanctioned alterations to the work . . . Alerted to the situation by a review of the show in the paper, Music Theatre International, which licenses the show, immediately contacted the [theatre] requesting a list of songs used in the production. Soon after receiving them, the organisation withdrew the rights for the production.

Stage, 19 April 2001

RECORDING A SHOW

If you wish to make a recording of a work which is copyright protected, your group will need permission. Most standard licences to perform plays and musicals do not grant such a right. This is because the agent is normally only allowed to deal with performance rights (or grand rights), and not film or sound-recording rights, which will usually be owned by or licensed to another body. In rare situations, a licence holder may be granted the right to make a recording for archival purposes only. Even with this permission, it would be a breach of copyright to make multiple copies. Some video production companies claim that they have a licence which covers this situation. This is likely to be a licence to video private functions, not a public performance.

The Act also grants a right to performers (including musicians). If a recording is made of the whole or a substantial part of a performance other than for private and domestic use without the performers' permission, then it is an infringing copy. Venue operators often insist that one of the terms on which tickets are sold is 'no recording' because they may be jointly liable for the infringement of the performers' right. This right is due to be strengthened by European legislation, but it is likely that the new rules will not be ready for many years.

CHARITY PERFORMANCES AND PRIVATE PERFORMANCES

All public performances of copyright-protected works require permission from the copyright owners. If a performance is in public, then it is covered by the Act, whether or not any admission charge is made, and whether or not any profit goes to charity. The copyright owner may be willing to reduce or waive their fee, but this is unlikely.

Performances which take place at home are likely to be 'private and domestic', unless strangers are invited to attend after paying an admission charge. Performances for members of clubs or in hospitals will probably be public performances, even if the audience is restricted to members or patients only. It may be worth checking – each case is decided on its own facts.

PERFORMING EXTRACTS

Even a public performance of an extract from a copyright-protected work is covered by the Act. Permission will be required even if you only want to use, for example, the overture to a musical, or one scene from a play. Again, the copyright owner may be willing to reduce or waive their fee for an extract. Non-dramatic excerpts from musicals, such as 'Songs from the Shows'-type concert performances, are covered by a collective licence scheme run by the Performing Rights Society (PRS). Most professional venues have a suitable licence, but always check. The licence has some strict conditions:

- the excerpt does not exceed twenty-five minutes
- it is not a complete act of the musical
- it is not a 'potted version' of the musical
- it is performed with no changes to the music or lyrics
- it is performed using published or authorised musical arrangements

- no scenery, costume, choreography, staging, character representation or special lighting is used

If your group cannot fulfil the terms of these conditions it will need to approach the author (or the author's agent) for specific permission.

COMPILATION MUSICALS

There has been a recent trend to produce musicals which bring together a number of songs written or performed by an individual or group (*Mamma Mia!*, *Buddy*) or a type of music (*Soul Train*, *Smoky Joe's Café*). If the show consists of a number of existing songs, albeit arranged in some form of narrative, there is some doubt as to whether this is one dramatic work which requires the consent of the composer, or whether they are to be treated as a series of separate performances of songs or non-dramatico-musical works for which the PRS can issue a licence. The PRS may choose to decline to issue a licence. It would then be necessary to approach the author for permission. For more details about the PRS and other licence requirements relating to music, see the section on sound effects and music on pages 172-6.

DATABASES

The creator of a database enjoys protection from unauthorised copying. For example, an agent may wish to produce a database of all the plays that the agent deals with. The content of the database is protected by copyright, and a group may not copy it without permission. Further protection was granted under the Copyright and Rights in Database Regulations 1997.

Freedom of Expression

Some people use the performing arts as a way of expressing strongly held personal views. Up until December 1968, the Lord Chamberlain was responsible for vetting all new scripts. Although the days of censorship have gone, the law still seeks to balance freedom of expression with the protection of public morals. That balance may shift following the introduction of the Human Rights Act, 1998, which confirms an individual's right to freedom of expression. Article 10 of the European Convention on Human Rights states:

> Everyone has the right to freedom of expression. This right shall include freedom to hold opinions and to receive and impart information and ideas without interference by public authority and regardless of frontiers.

But this right is heavily qualified and will be balanced with other conflicting duties and responsibilities.

Complying with the statutory framework may not be enough. Some shows may be too shocking for your audience, or unpalatable to your members. The local authority (as the authority responsible for licensing public performances) and other funders or sponsors may wish to comment on a controversial production. Discuss the show with the group's cast and crew who also may have strong views. Gauge the likely audience reaction, and be prepared to handle complaints.

Some shows may be too shocking for your audience.

OBSCENITY AND INDECENCY

If a play's effect, taken as a whole, is to 'tend to deprave and corrupt persons who are likely, having regard to all the relevant circumstances, to attend it' (from section 2, Theatres Act, 1968) a criminal offence has taken place. A shocking, vulgar or lewd show that may cause offence is not necessarily obscene. But sexual acts, taking drugs and encouraging violence have been found by the courts to be obscene.

The National Theatre's 1980 production of *The Romans in Britain* included a scene of simulated male rape. The theatre and the director were subject to a criminal charge under the Sexual Offences Act, 1956, of attempting to procure an act of gross indecency between two males. However, when the prosecution's evidence was shown to be unreliable, the case was dropped. Since 1982, a number of plays have been introduced with similar scenes (the National Theatre's production of *Angels in America* in 1992; Hampstead Theatre's 1994 production of *Alas Poor Superman* and, perhaps most notably, the Royal Court's production at the Ambassadors Theatre in 1996 of *Shopping and Fucking*). No action was taken, but the Sexual Offences Act could still be applied to stage performances.

The depiction of violence is similarly subject to a changing test. The stage for the 2001 production of *The Lieutenant of Inishmore* at the Other Place, Stratford-upon-Avon, was reported to be 'so slippery with gore that one member of the cast skidded as he took his curtain call' (Susannah Clapp, *Observer*, 20 May 2001). Recent guidance from the British Board of Film Classification reflects its belief that society has become more tolerant of material of a sexual nature, but it was not prepared to relax its strict stance on violence. Because obscenity is a criminal offence, extreme caution should be exercised. If in doubt, obtain legal advice.

Indecency is a separate offence, but a general exception exists for the performance of a 'play'. However, this exception does not include front-of-house material or publicity photographs. Naked or near-naked bodies, if in context, may not cause concern to the majority of adult audiences if warnings are given on publicity, at the time the ticket was purchased and prior to the show. However, check for local by-laws – Nottingham, for example, has a local law which prohibits nude performances. Away from the controlled environment of a theatre auditorium, where the venue management have some control over the membership of an audience, standards will be different. The criminal offences of committing an act which outrages public decency or indecent exposure may apply to some seriously risqué street theatre.

Language or other themes normally restricted on television to after the 9 p.m. watershed can be presented, but again, suitable warnings should be considered. Some of the classics may need special consideration: Tennessee Williams's *Vieux Carré* includes a violent scene of a sexual nature that could shock. More recently: Dave Simpson's comedy, *Girls' Night Out*, includes characters who are performing male strippers. Special care should be taken if the show's content includes or makes reference to indecency in relation to children.

RACIAL HATRED

If a public performance of a play is given which involves the use of threatening, abusive or insulting words or behaviour [such as to stir up racial hatred], the person who presents or directs the performance is guilty of [a criminal] offence.

from the Public Order Act, 1986, section 20

Voluntary equal opportunity policies may include broader controls so always check for conditions, especially when hiring property owned by or licensed by local authorities. Actions that may not amount to racial hatred may nevertheless cause ill feeling with members of local communities of a particular race. For this reason, many local authorities have decided not to license public performances which involve cast members blacking up.

BREACH OF THE PEACE

If a performance provokes an uproar, or other disturbance which might cause injury to people or property, the group or its director may be arrested and charged with a breach of the peace. The actors will not be liable to prosecution if they have followed the directions given to them. At a minimum, expect the show to be closed down.

DEFAMATION

If a show contains references to real living people, and those references could cause damage or injury to reputation, property or goodwill, the script might be libellous (Defamation Act 1996). If the person concerned has not granted permission for the reference, seek legal advice before the performance.

BLASPHEMY

The law of blasphemy applies only to England and Wales. It relates to any material that vilifies, or is contemptuous of, or which denies the truth of the Christian religion, the Bible or the Book of Common Prayer. If a show contains material which would outrage the feelings of the general body of Christians, then a criminal offence is committed. To question the existence of God or to express hostile opinions will not amount to blasphemy.

The Actors

CASTING

Most groups will experience a level of competition between members for the leading roles in each production, and your group must decide on a fair and efficient way of choosing between those people. As in all competitions, there will be winners and losers, and some people will feel hurt or angry that they have not been chosen for a particular role. This is a natural reaction, and your group should respond by making the process as fair and as stress-free as possible. Auditions are a way of selecting the right person for each acting part. Remember that the audition may be one of the first contacts that potential members make with your group. If the process is too daunting, your group is unlikely to see that person again.

WHO CAN AUDITION?

It may be necessary to decide upon some entry criteria for auditions. Some groups specify that anyone who wishes to audition must be a fully paid-up member of the group. This encourages everyone to be involved in the group's wider activities, but needs to be carefully balanced against the impression of elitism. 'Open auditions' are sessions during which anyone is welcome to volunteer. These are especially useful if the group is encouraging new recruits to take part. Consider preparing a statement so that the process is clear:

For each show, a cast is selected by open audition by a panel of at least [four] people. Parts will be awarded based only on the requirements of the show and the performance of the person at audition.

WHAT HAPPENS AT AN AUDITION?

Typically, each volunteer is called into a private room, and asked to perform extracts from the show. If the show is a musical, the actor may be asked to read an extract from the script, sing and perhaps perform a dance routine. The extracts should be carefully chosen to give the performer the opportunity to present as many of the facets of the role or character as possible.

In order to give everyone an equal chance, a list of the extracts that will be used at the audition should be made available well in advance, together with a brief description of each role and any special requirements. To avoid embarrassment later in the rehearsal process, reference should be made to any sensitive issues. For example, make it clear if a particular character takes part in any action of a sexual nature, or if the actor will be required to appear naked or semi-naked on stage. It would not be normal to ask someone to strip at an audition.

Also consider whether more than one person will be required to perform each part – this may be necessary for junior members of the cast who may not be able to perform on consecutive nights.

There may be times when a less structured audition process would be better. If the show requires improvisation, or needs a small cast, it may be better to bring all the actors together, and allow them to read through a script, or take part in some improvisation exercises so that a decision can be made based on the group's dynamics. For small parts, it may be acceptable not to audition actors at all, but to allot these parts to the actors during rehearsals. Whatever the method, it should be made clear to all participants, and not changed without full consultation. Group work may be seen as less daunting, especially for new members.

CASTING DECISIONS

The group as a whole will always have the final say, but casting is often delegated to the governing body, who may in turn delegate to a subcommittee. The director will always be present, and may have the casting vote on all decisions. If your group has a choreographer and musical director, they should also be present. Some groups also include an 'independent' members' representative to ensure the process is fair.

Everyone will want to know the decisions of the audition panel as soon as possible after the auditions. Offer the parts to the successful actors, and let them know as much as possible about the rehearsal process, to ensure that the actors will be fully aware of the commitment that is expected from them before they accept or decline the offered part. If no decision can be made, let the affected actors know, and give a timetable to resolve the outstanding issues.

REHEARSALS

To transform a script into an engaging performance takes time, and rehearsals provide the opportunity to discover, explore and craft the theatrical art. Rehearsals allow the actors to become familiar with their roles and the structure of the show as a whole. The director will be able to instruct, mould and nurture each character so that when the show is performed in front of an audience, everyone involved will know exactly what is expected of them.

For amateur groups, rehearsal time is also a social occasion. People will naturally want to talk, and this may be the time when people catch up on friendships. A director may need to judge when to call a group to order, to maintain a working atmosphere. To keep actors interested, the group should agree a rehearsal timetable, asking only those actors who are required for the scenes being rehearsed to attend. If time is tight, it may be possible for rehearsals to be split –

with different members rehearsing different parts of the show at the same time.

Rehearsal space may also be at a premium. Try to use a space which is at least as large as the performance space. Indicate on the floor the size of the space, and provide furniture and props to help the actors become used to the action on stage.

During the rehearsal period, time must also be allotted for discussion with the technicians. All backstage helpers should be aware of the general demands of the show and the particular issues that have been raised during the rehearsals. Key members of the technical team should be present during the final rehearsals so that they are familiar with the action on stage.

The rehearsal schedule should also include some time at the performance venue. If hired for one week, it may be possible to arrange the get-in and a technical rehearsal on the first day, followed by a full dress rehearsal on the second. This allows a performance period of five days. Whatever the period, it is likely that not everything will go to plan, and that nerves will be stretched. Careful planning at an early stage will keep these situations to a minimum, but always allow some time for the unexpected.

Children

Working with children and young people, contrary to a commonly held view, can be very rewarding. However, to encourage participation, your group will need to consider the special needs of its younger members. Making specific arrangements takes time and effort, which may be in short supply. But a group will only continue to thrive if it attracts new, younger members to replace those who are no longer active participants.

THE NEEDS OF CHILDREN

A group which attracts young members should be willing to accept the responsibility for their welfare while they are involved in the group's activities. Some of the inherent risks that may be obvious to the more experienced members will appear to be new and exciting to children. The first concern for the group must therefore be the safety of its members, with special consideration given to those younger members who are unskilled or lack experience.

Remember that young members will be subject to the stresses and strains of the education system, and the need to revise for examinations will press hard on their spare time. If necessary, liaise with the local schools to make sure that the demands of any rehearsal timetable are realistic. Late-night rehearsals are not acceptable for children, at any time of the year.

The group's duty of care will not end when a rehearsal or performance finishes. It may also extend to ensuring that the child returns to his or her parent or guardian safely. Discuss travel arrangements, and make sure the group has some way of contacting the parent or guardian in unforeseen circumstances.

There are many other ways of involving younger members in the group's activities. Local schools or youth groups may jump at the chance of being involved in a joint project.

One group worked with students at the local college who were studying make-up. Although they had worked with photographers, they wanted experience of the different demands of stage make-up. Several of the students volunteered to help for a production of *Scrooge* which is set in Victorian times. Some of the cast were more than happy to arrive a few minutes early to give these students a chance to apply false hair and stage make-up. The results were up to our usual standards, and the students went on to work with the theatre's own staff on other performances.

PARENT OR GUARDIAN CONSENT

Provide parents and guardians with clear information about the group, and a description of the group's activities. Supply a 'permission form', which can be completed by the carer, as a permanent record on file that the parent/guardian understands the group's activities, and consents to their child being involved in those activities. The form could also include space for emergency contact details. Since the imposition of medical treatment without consent can amount to a criminal assault, groups should consider asking for specific consent from the parent or guardian to any necessary emergency medical treatment in the event that the carer cannot be contacted.

For special events, such as trips to other theatres, additional consents should be sought. Consider checking with the carer whether the child suffers from allergies, requires medication, has suffered from any recent illnesses, has any dietary requirements and any other details relevant to the planned event. This should help prevent unexpected accidents.

REDUCING THE RISK OF ABUSE

It is a sad fact that a small number of children are subject to abuse by other children or adults. There is an ever present risk that some adults may be attracted to theatre groups in order to gain contact with these children. Complacency about these issues is a totally inadequate response and your group should maintain a proper level of awareness supported by a clear policy.

A group can reduce the risk of abuse by following a policy which makes effective arrangements for the supervision of children. Children should not be left unattended, and should normally be supervised by at least two adults. Try to create good communication between the group and the children to encourage them to raise any issues that are concerning them.

If you suspect abuse, consult members of your governing body immediately (unless those people may be involved). Do not act alone or try to investigate the situation. Do not delay reporting suspicions. Make careful notes. If the managing body decides to take action, they should speak to a social worker or a member of the police force's child protection team. If a child is in immediate danger, use the 999 emergency number. Other contact details are given in the Reference Section at the end of the handbook.

THE CRIMINAL RECORDS BUREAU

It is difficult for voluntary groups to access the present system of checking the suitability of volunteers. In addition to the police force, details are currently held by the Department of Health under the Protection of Children Act 1999 (the PoCA list) and the Department for Education and Employment (List 99). Some local authorities will access this information on behalf of voluntary groups, and guidance is available from the Department of Health via their help line. However, a new system was proposed by the Police Act, 1997, which is due to start in late 2001 or early 2002. The new process is known as Disclosure, which is provided by the Criminal Records Bureau. It aims to provide a one-stop service for access to records held by police, Department of Health and the Department for Education and Employment. Voluntary groups will be able to ask a person wishing to work with children to apply for a certificate from the Bureau for free. The Bureau issues three types of certificate. A criminal conviction certificate covers unspent convictions only. A criminal record certificate lists spent and unspent convictions, but these will only be available to bodies who have registered with the Bureau. For work involving unsupervised access to children, the Bureau will produce an enhanced criminal record certificate which also includes cautions and other information from the police. Where relevant, the certificate will include details from the PoCA list and List 99. Under the Criminal Justice and Court Services Act, 2000, it is an offence for an individual to knowingly offer work, or allow someone to continue to work in a regulated position if that person appears on one of the lists. Regulated positions include unsupervised contact with children arranged by a parent or guardian; training or supervising positions and trustees of children's charities.

LOCAL AUTHORITY LICENCES

Before a child (which is defined in this context as anyone under the age of sixteen) is allowed to perform, his or her health, welfare and education must be addressed to the satisfaction of the local authority. In most situations, a licence must be obtained in accordance with the Children and Young Persons Act, 1963, the Children (Performances) Regulations, 1968 (amended in 1998 and 2000), and the Children (Protection at Work) Regulations, 1998 (amended twice in 2000). In Scotland, the Children and Young Persons (Scotland) Act, 1937, and the Children Protection at Work (Scotland) Regulations, 2000, apply. The regulations include a complete prohibition on any child taking part in a performance in which 'his/her life or limbs are endangered'. They also include provision for:

- medical examinations
- local authority-approved chaperones
- approval of rehearsal and performance space
- approval of travelling arrangements
- a requirement that the child's education should not suffer
- the maximum number, time and frequency of performances and rehearsals
- the control of heavy work

Beware, since an application for a licence must be made to the local authority which deals with the child's home or boarding school at least twenty-one days before the date of the first performance. The application is made by the group, and countersigned by the child's parent or guardian. Not only will full details and photos need to be submitted with the application, but full records will need to be kept by the group in case the local authority checks that all the terms and conditions of the licence have been fulfilled.

The Acts contain a number of exceptions for amateur performances including:

- school productions
- performances if during the previous six months, the child has not taken part in other performances on more than three days

as long as the child does not take time off school. Again, the exceptions are complex, and detailed guidance should be sought.

The courts are strict when dealing with a child's well-being. There is an overriding duty to ensure that the welfare of the child is paramount. If a licence is not applied for, false details given on the application form, the conditions of the licence are not followed, or records not kept, the parent and the persons responsible for the production may be committing a criminal offence and be liable to a fine and/or imprisonment.

If in doubt, contact your local authority's education department in plenty of time. Many local authorities have local by-laws which may be more stringent than the national regulations. They may be able to provide you with guidance and a simplified application procedure if there are a number of children taking part.

CHILDREN AGED UNDER EIGHT

If your group works with children aged under eight years old, it may be required to register with the local authority as a provider of day care for children. The local authority will make checks to ensure that the people running the group are suitable, that the premises used are satisfactory and safe, and that other people employed on the premises are fit to be near children. Authorities levy a fee and require annual inspections. Generally, registration is not required if each session lasts less than two hours. However, holiday clubs or playschemes for children under eight, which take place for more than six days in any one year, will be required to register.

New regulations contained in the Care Standards Act, 2000, will come into force in September 2002. When fully implemented, the Act makes provision for the regulation of child-minding and the provision of day care in England under Her Majesty's Chief Inspector of Schools.

Musicians

INTRODUCTION

Many successful groups have members who are musicians, but even the most resourceful will on occasion need to engage some professional musicians to supplement or strengthen their orchestras, and many groups engage professional bands. The advantages of doing so are many. There is a good chance that a professional band will have played the score to your show before and this will limit the amount of time needed for rehearsals. In turn, this frees up the musical director to maximise the time that s/he spends working with the cast and chorus. The sheer complexity and difficulty of the music in some shows puts it beyond the capability of all but the most talented of amateur musicians.

Most musical directors will have contacts with local professional musicians – if not, the local branch of the Musicians' Union (MU) can help. Most localities will have a musician who acts as a 'fixer' and can introduce the group to suitable professional musicians. On occasion, the fixer may contract directly with the group for a global fee and then hire the individuals him or herself.

It is crucial when hiring professional musicians that the terms of the agreement are properly recorded. The Union publishes a number of standard contracts for use in all types of engagements. The relevant contracts in this sphere of work are:

- number 4 (for the engagement of an orchestra for engagements in theatres, typically used between a group and fixer)
- number 4a (for the engagement of individual musicians for engagements in

theatres, typically used between a fixer or group and an individual musician)

- number 8a (for the engagement of an individual musician for theatrical performances in non-theatrical venues)

Copies of all these contracts are available free of charge from the live engagements department at the Union's National Office.

Productions in many professional venues are covered by the MU's agreement with the Theatrical Managers Association (TMA). It is an obligation of membership that the TMA/MU agreement is used as the basis for paying musicians (except, of course, where the venue is let for bona fide amateur productions and the musicians are not receiving payment). Copies of these agreements are also available from the Union's offices. The current agreement (in force until 31 March 2002) includes the following provisions:

- Musicians are engaged on a weekly salary of £300 per week which allows them to be called for up to eight sessions (each lasting no more than three hours).
- The first week of a production ('production week') may consist of five or more sessions, with salary reduced pro rata. This is useful for groups producing, for example, grand opera that may only perform for, say, three nights plus two rehearsals.
- Additional calls over the eight (or five) are paid at £37.50 per session.
- Musicians playing a second instrument ('doubling') receive a supplement of 20% and those playing three instruments ('trebling') receive a supplement of 30%.
- A number of additional payments are made, which include holiday pay at $1/12$ of salary per week worked, paid at the end of the engagement; travel payments (for journeys over twenty-five miles each way from home to the venue); 'porterage' (transportation) of large instruments; and on-stage payments.

For productions in venues other than theatres and cinemas (i.e. school or parish halls) the fees are the same as the TMA/MU but the maximum number of sessions per week is six, rather than eight, with salaries reduced pro rata. Most other conditions apply.

Most Scottish venues are members of the Federation of Scottish Theatre. The current standard agreement between these two organisations is currently under review (2001), so check with the venue to ascertain which trade agreement applies.

MEDIA ISSUES

Many groups are keen to achieve some free publicity on television and radio and the MU has 'News Access' provisions to cater for this. Under the News Access code, television cameras etc. may be allowed into a dress rehearsal or performance to record for publicity purposes. In this situation the musician does not receive an additional fee. Broadcasters are limited to one minute of featured use and one minute of non-featured use (i.e. in the background with the interviewer talking at the same time), which should be sufficient to meet the needs of most 'what's on'-type slots in regional news programmes.

Subject to copyright restrictions, archive recordings can be made for non-commercial purposes, provided the MU is informed at least seven days before the recording is due to be made. Such recordings should only be of the quality necessary for a record of the performance, that is, shot with a single camera from a fixed position. Recordings made for sale to the public attract additional fees: further information can be obtained from the Union's media department at National Office.

FUNDING

The Musicians' Union, through its Music Promotion Committee, gives guarantees against loss to amateur productions using MU members of up to £1,000 per production. For orchestras and bands of twelve MU members or more, up to 10% of orchestra costs can be awarded and for orchestras of eighteen or more, up to 15% of orchestra costs. The group will be asked to acknowledge the Union's financial assistance in programmes or other publicity material.

Additionally, the Performing Rights Society Foundation aims to distribute up to £1 million per year to support all types of new music and related activities.

Animals

The group is under a duty to protect any animals used in a show from any unnecessary cruelty, abuse or injury. Regulations are set out in the Performing Animals (Regulations) Act, 1925, and the Dangerous Wild Animals Act, 1976. The first provides that no one may 'exhibit' or 'train' an animal for performance unless registered by the relevant local authority. The second requires persons keeping specified animals to hold a licence. Registration may be revoked or be subject to further conditions if the techniques used are found to be cruel. Using a reputable handler will reduce any risk. Some agencies are members of the Animal Consultants and Trainers Association (ACTA). Always check with your local authority to ensure you can meet their requirements early in the planning stages. If a certificate is not obtained, the person in charge could be subject to a criminal conviction.

If in doubt, also check with the RSPCA. They advocate that an animal should not do anything that does not come naturally to its species or breed. The RSPCA prefers to see alternatives used, whenever possible. Consider whether the animal need appear on stage at all, or whether a toy or puppet can be used instead. If no alternatives are possible, use the following checklist:

- Let the cast and crew know early that an animal is going to be used. Some people have phobias, others are allergic to some animals. The animal's bedding, especially if soiled, may be hazardous. Be very careful if a member of your group is pregnant.
- Carry out a written risk assessment. A good source of advice will be the owner or trainer. Be aware that you will be less familiar with the animal than

its full-time handler. It may be helpful to talk to a vet. Consider what harm the animal could cause and what harm the animal could suffer. What contact will there be with the animal? Who will be exposed to the risk? What other animals may be present? What could go wrong?

- Make a member of the group responsible for the welfare of the animal, including feeding and watering arrangements. Perform basic hygiene routines. Ensure people know what to do in an emergency. Keep details of veterinary care and first-aid arrangements.
- Provide suitable housing, which should be at a comfortable temperature in a quiet place. Give the animal adequate rest periods, away from the venue. It may be necessary to use more than one animal if there is more than one show per day.
- Keep the time span the animal will be used to a minimum. If possible, rehearse last and perform first.
- Fireproof any bedding used on stage. If this is not possible, agree suitable alternatives with the fire officer.
- If the group is going to purchase the animal, first check it will have a good home to go to after the show's run.

Be prepared for bad publicity. Some animal rights organisations are against the use of live animals for performances. If demonstrations at the venue are possible, inform the police.

Animals: provide suitable housing, which should be at a comfortable temperature in a quiet place.

Rehearsal and Performance Venues

INTRODUCTION

Performance spaces do not need to be specially designed and built. Shows can take place in the most unusual of places. Some groups are lucky enough to own a venue. Others arrange to share a performance space. A few create their own. Some groups specialise in performing outdoors or in public spaces. Others tour from venue to venue. Although the size and shape of the performance space will be important to the director and designer of a particular show, the number of seats in the auditorium will be equally important to the group's finance manager. The seating capacity is directly related to the possible income the group will receive to help pay for the expenses of putting on the show.

As well as a performing space, a group may need areas for rehearsals and storage. These need not be in the same building, although some time and energy may be saved if all are located near to each other.

STORAGE SPACE

If the group has large amounts of costume, props or scenery, it will need a storage space. Most groups start by using a member's spare room, shed or garage. Sometimes this can be awkward, especially if that member leaves the group. These informal arrangements may also make it difficult to obtain insurance cover for the group's belongings.

Although storage space need not be near the performing space, or the majority of the members, long trips to the store take time and cost money. When checking possible locations, also check that vehicles can reach the store easily – the nearer large trucks can get to the store, the easier it will be to collect and deliver scenery.

The more space the group requires, the more expensive it is likely to be. Check not just the floor space, but also the height of the ceiling – if sets are being constructed, plenty of headroom is a bonus. While checking ceilings, also check the state of the roof – if the building is not waterproof, measures will be needed to protect delicate items.

If the space is to be used to construct sets, a source of electricity for power tools (and kettle!) is a minimum requirement. Check who is responsible for paying the electricity bill and whether it is a fixed fee included in the rent.

Lastly, consider security for the building – how many other people could gain access?

A group in Manchester were concerned about security, and asked their local police force for advice. They recommended improvements to locks and alarms that qualified the group for discounts on their insurance policy.

REHEARSAL SPACE

Initial meetings to talk about a show or perhaps to read through scripts often take place in a member's home. However, most groups will need to have regular access to a rehearsal space. To encourage attendance, the space should be easily accessible, so consider car parking, public transport and generally how safe the area feels. If members or potential members have any special needs, make sure you consider these factors.

The rehearsal space should be at least as large as the performing area, so that everyone gets used to the dimensions of the stage. Rehearsals can be noisy, especially dance rehearsals or singing rehearsals. Will this noise upset other users of the building or neighbours? Conversely, will noise from outside the rehearsal space affect the concentration of the members? Other facilities may be required – toilets and access to refreshments should be readily available, and help the rehearsal process to be a more social event.

PERFORMANCE SPACE

A director will need to have some indication of the size of the performing area before rehearsals commence. Try to obtain scale drawings of the stage, or at least some basic measurements to help the director, designer and set builders. Also try to obtain details of the whole performance space, not just the stage. These details should include the backstage and front-of-house facilities. The location of the venue is also important, not just for the members, but also the audience. Consider accessibility to the venue and to the auditorium. Some professional theatres or local authorities have disability officers who can provide advice on accessibility issues.

If the performance space is not a permanent theatre, special care will need to be taken. Although staging, lighting and sound systems can be hired, many more factors need considering:

- acoustics (will the audience be able to hear the performance?)
- sight lines (will the audience be able to see the performance?)
- safety (is there sufficient room? fire exits? fire-fighting equipment?)
- power (stage lighting requires lots of electricity)
- seating (position? number? comfort?)
- accessibility
- car parking

Open-air performances are even more difficult, and these are covered in more depth in Part 1.

A group in the south-west lost their regular performance venue when the building was redeveloped. They raised enough funds to purchase their own space and approached the Independent Theatre

Council and the Association of British Theatre Technicians for guidance to ensure that their new space met all statutory requirements.

The Association of British Theatre Technicians has published *Technical Standards for Places of Entertainment*, which is expected to become a reference for licensing authorities.

HIRING A SPACE

A landowner ('landlord') may be willing to grant your group the right to use land and buildings for storage, rehearsal or performance. In return, it is likely that the group will have to give the landlord some legally binding promises, including the promise to pay rent, and to leave the property on an agreed date in the same state it was found. Before any agreement is entered into, the group's constitution or rule book should be checked to make sure it has the power to enter into these types of arrangement. Also consider obtaining advice from experts, including:

- valuation of the property/level of rent from a specialist estate agent or valuer
- a structural survey by a chartered surveyor
- legal advice to check the landowner's right to enter into the agreement and whether the property can be used for its intended purpose. The building may need planning permission, probably a local authority licence, and must be clear of other legal restrictions
- independent financial advice, especially if the group requires borrowing to fund the arrangement

LEASES AND LICENCES

There are two types of legally binding arrangement that could apply if your group hires a venue. These arrangements are called 'leases' and 'licences', and are collectively called 'lettings'. A lease will grant more rights than a licence, and so the distinction is important. Unfortunately, a group cannot always rely on the name given to the arrangement by the parties – if the agreement is challenged, a court will look beyond the headings used. The following is only a summary of the law relating to land and buildings, which is a complex area. Your group must obtain legal advice on specific arrangements.

A 'lease' will only be legally binding if it meets certain criteria. Leases are often used if the landlord (the lessor) wishes to grant a group (the lessee) exclusive use of the building for an agreed fixed period of time (the term). In return, the lessee may be required to pay rent and fulfil other obligations (covenants), which may include repairing and insuring the property. A lease may be transferred to another tenant (subject to the landlord's approval).

'Exclusive use' means that no one else can use the property during the term. It also means that the group can keep everyone else out. However, the landlord often retains the right to check the property or enter the building in an emergency.

A lease may need to be made by a formal document (deed) if it is to be a binding agreement. Statutory rules exist for business leases of more than six months in England and Wales. Charities and voluntary groups are included in the statutory definition of 'business'. These rules mean that a lease or tenancy can be automatically extended in certain situations.

A Suffolk-based drama group was granted a two-year lease by a farmer for a barn to store scenery and large props. At the end of the term, the farmer changed the locks and refused the group access to the barn. The group took legal advice and gained access to the barn for a further period.

Don't be surprised if the lease agreement is printed in duplicate. If so, the lease will be signed by the landlord and retained by the group, and the duplicate (or counterpart) will be signed by the group and retained by the landlord.

If the group does not have exclusive control of the property, so that others are allowed access to the land and buildings during the rental term, then the arrangement will probably not be a lease, but rather a licence. The agreement will be a personal arrangement between the owner (licensor) and the group (licensee). Unless agreement is reached to the contrary, the owner will be entitled to use the property and allow others to do so at times when the property is not contractually required to be available to the licensee.

The differences between leases and licences are sometimes hard to spot, and even the most informal arrangement may at law be a lease. If in doubt, do not rely on the description on the face of the document, but seek legal advice to study the particular terms of the agreement. Remember that the distinction may be very important, because some types of protection are only available to groups who enter into leases and not licences.

Most arrangements for hiring a venue for performances will be licences. The owners of a venue will keep overall control of the building, with permission granted to the licensee to use parts of the building (the stage, dressing rooms, green room, scenery store, technical areas and orchestra pit) during certain times of the day. It is likely that the venue operator will keep control over the auditorium, administrative offices and front-of-house. Most licences should include the following information:

- **Parties**: This relates to the people or organisations that are entering into the arrangement, rather than the after-show celebrations!
- **Cost**: This is one of the fundamental terms of the agreement – how much will it cost to hire the venue? The charge may be calculated on an hourly, daily or weekly rate, or on the number of performances given. It may be calculated as a percentage of the box-office receipts (although this is more common for the professional theatre). Check if the quoted cost includes VAT or not. Check to see if a deposit is payable. Check to see if extra costs can be charged, for example, for providing box-office facilities.
- **Times and dates**: The agreement should set out the exact time and date that the arrangements start and finish, together with the times that the venue will be available each day.

- **Security**: Will the landlord require some form of confirmation that the group will pay the rent, and look after the property? Sometimes a deposit is required, or alternatively, that named individuals guarantee the obligations of the group.
- **Access**: Is it clear what is meant by the 'venue'? Does it include all or only part of the building? Does the group have access to all the areas it requires? Check the route from the public highway to ensure all rights of access are granted. Be careful that they include fire escape routes and, if relevant, access to toilets, parking and loading bays. Does the venue operator retain the right to allow others to use the venue?
- **Provision of services**: The venue's management will normally pay for heating, lighting and cleaning. The cost of electricity can be debatable, especially if the venue is not designed to power theatre lighting, etc., so make sure the agreement makes the position clear. The venue's management may also pay to insure the building but not the group's belongings. Sometimes the venue will also supply stage equipment, personnel or box-office facilities.
- **Care of the venue**: In addition to paying the agreed fee, the group will have to comply with any rules set out in the agreement, or other documents referred to in the agreement. This is likely to include health and safety measures. The group will probably have to promise to look after the building and not cause any damage. This is especially important in the stage area, and if the group defaults, it could be facing large repair costs.
- **Licensing**: The group might have to promise the venue management that they have permission to perform the show. Check whether the venue has suitable public entertainment, liquor and other licences required for the performance.
- **Intervals**: The agreement may impose penalties if the show does not have intervals, because the venue will lose profits from food and drink sales.
- **Marketing**: The venue owner may require some control over the wording of tickets and the marketing of the show. The venue operator may want to include rules relating to the sale of merchandise.
- **Default**: The agreement should set out what happens if the group cancels the show, or if the venue becomes unavailable. Will the venue operator require some form of comfort that the group will pay the rent and look after the property? Sometimes a deposit is required or, alternatively, that named

individuals guarantee the obligations of the group.

- **Arbitration**: The agreement may show that both parties are happy to use mediation or arbitration schemes rather than resort to litigation if there is a dispute.

In most cases, it will be obvious who the landlord will be, but if the group is dealing with a stranger, it may be worth checking the credentials of the landlord. If a group wishes to use a church hall, it should check whether permission can be granted by the incumbent, the church wardens or the parochial church council. Similarly, village halls may be run by a local committee or trustees. Registered charities, limited companies and limited partnerships are obliged to file records, which are accessible to the public.

IF THE AGREEMENT IS BREACHED

If everything goes wrong, and a venue manager ends the agreement without justification, a group may be able to successfully claim a cash sum to cover its losses. Any agreement should clearly state what types of loss the venue would be responsible for. In any event, making a claim through the courts is costly, time-consuming and risky. The group should check to see if any amicable settlement is possible. If not, both parties may be prepared to enter into mediation or arbitration. Some costs, including cancellation costs, may be covered by the group's insurance policy.

If the group cancels, it is likely (depending on the exact terms of the agreement) to lose any deposit and may be liable to pay the full amount of the agreed rental fee plus an amount to cover the disruption caused. If the venue cannot find a replacement for the cancelled show, it may be able to claim for the overheads of the venue for that period.

Depending on the governing documents of the group, the members of unincorporated associations who enter into these types of agreement on behalf of a group may be personally liable to the landlord if any of the promises made by the group are broken. If the group defaults, the landlord may have the right to ask those particular members who entered into the arrangement on behalf of the group to make good the broken promise. In some situations, the members who enter into the arrangement may be able to claim a contribution from other officers of the group, or all of the other members. Further details of members' liabilities are on pages 234-6. Any individual should consider obtaining independent legal advice before agreeing to rent property on behalf of a group.

BUYING A PERFORMANCE SPACE

Before buying property, the group's rules and regulations will need to be reviewed to see if the group has the power to purchase land, especially if the group is an unincorporated association. Consult with the professionals listed on pages 122-3.

If your group is very fortunate, it may be given a suitable property. Yes, it does happen! Throughout this section, references are made to the Lantern Theatre, in Sheffield:

> We were very lucky when, in 1957, our founder Dilys Guite discovered the almost derelict Chalet Theatre. The owner had for many years been looking for someone who wanted to put it back into use as a theatre, rather than develop the land. She struck a deal with the owner and paid a small rent while she and some of her friends went to work on the neglected buildings and grounds. After several months of very hard work repairing and renovating the theatre, it reopened in November 1957 as the renamed Lantern Theatre.
>
> The owner was so impressed with their work and enthusiasm that the owner gave the theatre, adjoining stables and the land to the Dilys Guite Players in memory of his wife. The stables are now used as a dressing room, wardrobe and storage. The land is now our car park. Over the years this very generous gift has saved us a lot of money, by not having to pay rent, and is probably one of the main reasons that the group is still able to survive.

Buying land is a complicated transaction, and can take some considerable time. Don't rely on informal promises or representations. Check everything before the group is committed to purchasing the building. Don't just leave an inspection to the surveyor – members of the group should also attend to make sure the property meets with the group's requirements. Tackle any issues raised by these reports as soon as possible, and don't be afraid of walking away if it is not in the best interests of the group to proceed.

Special care should be taken if the property is being purchased from one of the members of the group. If that member is also a director of the group, special rules apply. Also check whether the transaction has any tax consequences – especially VAT.

A solicitor will complete some investigations, including a local search. This is a formal system of checking legal matters with the local authority. This includes information relating to planning permission. If the venue has been recently built or altered, that work should comply with building regulations. Given the nature of the use of the building, it would also be worthwhile checking with the local fire officer to ensure that there are no hidden costs in bringing the building up to date with current regulations. Once purchased, the advantages can be enjoyed:

> We put on five productions, each of six nights, between October and June. Owning the theatre means that we are free to build our set in the theatre over the six or seven weeks of the rehearsal period. This has advantages to both the cast and backstage crew because, well before the dress rehearsal, both know what the set will look like and which way doors, cupboards, windows, etc. open. If the director or cast find that the set is not easy to work with, we can make alterations and improvements as we go along and not have a mad rush when we get to the performance venue.
>
> All our properties, furniture, scenery and costumes are constructed and kept on the premises and not at members' houses. Having all the theatre property on site means that we can hire it out to other groups and individuals which means extra income.

Owning property does have its disadvantages:

There are so many jobs to be done, when you own your own theatre, that it keeps the members busy all year round. The theatre has to be kept in good repair and must be kept safe for both the group's members and the visiting public. This can be anything from replacing light bulbs to repairing leaking roofs. Larger jobs are completed by qualified contractors. The theatre must have all the necessary first aid, emergency lighting and fire equipment which must be serviced annually by a qualified engineer. We also have to keep the stage equipment up to date and this can be quite expensive when replacing lighting and sound equipment.

The theatre must be clean and tidy and the toilets and wash-rooms fully stocked. The audience will expect refreshments so we also need volunteers for the coffee bar during each performance as well as a front-of-house manager, stewards and programme sellers.

If a group is the owner of the building, it can benefit from hiring out the venue to other groups. The Lantern Theatre licenses its car park to a firm of local accountants and also encourages other organisations to use the venue:

Over the last four years we have been hiring out the theatre to other groups, companies and individuals in the area for a variety of functions. These have included birthday parties, retirement parties, business meetings, rehearsals, auditions and performances of plays, concerts and musicals.

This has increased the income for the group and some people in the area who have never been to the Lantern to see one of our productions have found out about our performances and have subsequently been to see our plays.

Before allowing other organisations to use your group's facilities, check to make sure that they are competent – consider completing a full health and safety assessment with each new hirer. If they are inexperienced, consider supplying people with the relevant skills (at an extra fee). Also check with the group's insurers to see if they require any specific action.

One big advantage for the cast and stage crew is that on the last night we do not have to rush to get our set and properties out of the theatre and we can stay in the theatre and unwind with a last-night party, which can go on until we are ready to go home. The work can wait till the next day. While owning a theatre does have some disadvantages, the advantages win hands down.

Public Entertainment Licensing

In an attempt to regulate health and safety issues, it is now illegal to use premises for public performances of plays without a local authority licence, unless one of a limited number of exemptions applies. Some performances outside London that take place as part of a carnival or fête or religious gathering do not require performance licences, but your group will still be under the same duties of care to its members and audience, and will be subject to health and safety legislation. If in doubt, check with the local authority.

The first challenge is to make sure that the right licence regime applies – local authorities can grant a variety of licences and each has slightly different rules. Although the current government issued a consultation paper in late 2000 which outlined a simpler procedure, it is unlikely this will be in force for some time.

PUBLIC THEATRICAL PERFORMANCES

The current rules for theatrical performances for England and Wales are contained in the Theatres Act, 1968. The Act uses wide definitions, so that 'premises' includes outdoor venues, and 'plays' includes ballets. 'Public performances' include any performance to which the public are permitted access, whether they pay or not. Some private performances if given for private gain are also subject to the Act.

Applications are made to district councils, London borough councils or, in Wales, to the appropriate county council or county borough council which is responsible for the area in which the venue is situated. The appropriate body can grant a licence for the venue to cover a particular event ('occasional licence'), or for periods of up to a year. There is no standard application form, so check with your group's local authority.

Most local authorities have developed an application form which sets out the information that the authority requires. In all cases, the applicant must give at least fourteen to twenty-eight days' notice (depending on the type of licence). Always give the local authority as much notice as possible so that any problems can be dealt with. Your group may have to provide copies of the application to the local police or fire officer. The authority can set a 'reasonable' application fee and can also adopt its own application procedure. Fees may be reduced or waived if the event is organised by a charitable organisation or takes place in a community space.

Once granted, performances may take place on any day of the week. Some Sunday performances cannot start before 2 p.m. (except in London) and may be subject to special rules. The licence will be granted subject to conditions. Some authorities use standard terms and conditions, but these may be altered for individual circumstances. Conditions may include:

- layout of stage and seating
- fitting and testing safety curtains
- fireproofing of scenery, props, etc.
- provision of emergency lighting
- number of emergency exits, gangways and passages
- toilet facilities
- first-aid provision

Even if your group's proposed venue has a licence, it is worth checking it to make sure that all of the conditions can be fulfilled for your particular show. If not, it is possible to apply for a variation to the current terms of the licence. A breach of the conditions may mean that the current licence is revoked or suspended. An authorised officer of a licensing authority may at any reasonable time enter a venue to see if the conditions contained in a licence are being complied with. Fire officers or police officers have similar powers. Performing without a licence or breaking the terms of a licence is a criminal offence.

A 'private' performance will not, by definition, be a 'public' performance, and will not be subject to the same licensing regime. Although some guidance as to the meaning of 'private' has been given by the UK Courts, each case is decided on its merits. If in doubt, contact the copyright owner and explain the situation in detail. If the copyright owner agrees that a performance will be 'private', then no copyright licence fee is payable. It is also technically possible to operate a theatre 'club' from a venue which is only open to members. However, these types of clubs are still subject to liquor licensing, health and safety regulations and special rules relating to members clubs.

OTHER TYPES OF PUBLIC PERFORMANCE LICENCE

Because other licensing regimes exist, the Theatres Act states that it is not necessary to apply also for public music or dancing licences as long as these activities are part of the public theatrical performance. If a show is a mixed programme of musical entertainment, dancing and sketches, perhaps in the 'music-hall' genre, both a theatre licence and a public entertainment licence will be required. A public entertainment licence will also be required if music at the start, end and during the interval on any day exceeds one quarter of the time taken to perform the show.

If your group wants to include some computer-generated or filmed action (for example, in *Singin' in the Rain* or *City of Angels*) the group may also need a film exhibition licence.

Again, each type of public performance licence has its own application procedure and fees.

SELLING ALCOHOL

Before alcohol is sold or given to anyone who has paid an admission fee, it is necessary to obtain a liquor licence in accordance with the Licensing Act 1964 (as amended) and the Licensing (Occasional Permissions) Act 1933. These types of licences are granted by the licensing justices at the venue's local magistrates' court to one or more named individuals. Those named persons are responsible for making sure that the conditions of the licence are obeyed. There are different types of liquor licence:

- **occasional permissions**: for voluntary groups wishing to sell alcohol up to twelve times in any twelve-month period
- **occasional licences**: where an existing licence holder wishes to supply alcohol at different premises (for example, where a local public house runs a bar at a special event)
- **club registration certificates**: if alcohol is sold at a members club to genuine members of that club
- **justices' on licence**: for typical public houses and (with specific restrictions) other groups wishing to supply alcohol regularly

Perhaps even more confusingly, for England and Wales, if a theatre licence is in force, the venue does not need a licence for the sale of intoxicating liquor before, during and immediately after a performance if proper notice has been given to the clerk to the magistrates.

Some buildings cannot be used to supply alcohol, and it will be necessary to seek permission from a group's landlord or the property's previous owners. Charities are also subject to special rules since the sale of alcohol (on its own) cannot be a charitable purpose.

Until recently we only put on thirty performances a year. This meant that a full theatre licence was very expensive. Instead, we apply each time we are putting on a performance for an occasional entertainment and theatre licence. This can mean that the venue is checked to see if it is safe for public use and that we have the correct fire equipment and emergency lights and that they are all in good working order. It is a condition of the licence that the premises and emergency equipment have to be checked each time that we are open to the public to make sure that everything is in the correct place and has not been tampered with.

Recently, at the request of members and audience, we have been selling alcoholic drinks on selected nights. We cannot get a full liquor licence, so we have to apply for an occasional permission. The magistrates can ask for the applicants to appear in person so they must be able to attend the court which might mean taking time off work. Alcohol can be provided free, but the cost cannot be included in any entrance fee or other charge. Check that your group's constitution or venue owner does not prohit the provision of sale of alcohol. Special rules exist for charities.

FORTHCOMING CHANGES

It may come as some relief to know that the public entertainment licensing system and the liquor licensing rules are under review. It is likely that the new system will combine all of the various elements of the current licensing system into one application to the relevant local authority. However, even if the new rules are not delayed, they are unlikely to apply until 2004.

Licensing authorities are also reviewing their decision-making processes following the introduction of the Human Rights Act: not only must their decisions be legal, but they must be compatible with the European Convention on Human Rights (and particularly the right to peaceful enjoyment of property without undue interference from the state). The Home Office has recommended that every local authority review their fee structure and standard conditions to make sure they are 'defensible and proportionate' and 'relevant . . . [to] achieve the objectives . . . without adding unnecessary burdens'. It should be noted that the local authority is not responsible for policing the Disability Discrimination Act. Conditions relating solely to access on the grounds of disability may be challenged in the future for not being strictly relevant to health and safety.

Marketing

Marketing is about using a whole host of different techniques to attract larger or more diverse audiences, find new members and perhaps increasing income. It is a good idea for someone in the group to have overall responsibility and control of marketing, but it is a task that could involve everyone. Getting a good-sized audience benefits everyone, and marketing can be fun.

I've heard an old saying quoted by many marketing departments in theatres around the country: 'If a show sells, it's because it's a good show. If it doesn't sell, blame the marketing.' Whoever takes on the overall responsibility for marketing needs to have a thick skin, as well as a lot of imagination!

STRATEGY

Having a marketing strategy means nothing more than planning marketing at the same time that your group decides which show to perform. In many professional theatres, the company spends almost as much on marketing as on the sets and costumes. Bear this in mind when your group sets its budgets for a show. Marketing experts often refer to the 'four Ps' – Product, Place, Price and Promotion, and this could be a useful framework for your group.

P for Product – choosing the show: Why does your group exist? Is it to make money? Is it to introduce as many new people to shows as possible? Is it because you want to give as many people as possible the chance to appear in your shows? Is it because you want to give new writers a chance to put on their shows? There are probably many reasons and all of these will have a bearing on the shows your group puts on stage.

P for Place – the venue: Think about where you are performing the show and the number of seats you have to fill. There may be no point putting on a brand-new show by an unknown writer in a 600-seat venue for a long run. The cast will get disillusioned if there are only fifty people in the audience each night. On the other hand, have some confidence in your group's abilities. If the group uses a 100-seat venue and has a fifty-strong cast, you should be able to fill the auditorium for more than one performance. Be realistic about what you can achieve.

P for Price – how much to charge for tickets: Whatever the reasons for putting on the show, your group needs to be confident that it can get an audience; that it is charging the right amount for admission and there are enough people who are willing and able to pay.

When the group is setting the ticket prices, check out what other groups and venues are doing. In a festival, there is probably an average price. Pitch your ticket price around the average, slightly higher if the group is confident and well known in the town, or lower if the group is putting on something that people haven't heard of. If the group sets targets for its ticket income, be realistic and even conservative about how many people will come and how much they will pay. If the show is a big hit, the group will be thrilled about exceeding the target. If it doesn't do as well as hoped, it will not be such a disappointment. It is a good idea to budget for concession prices depending on whom you expect to attract. Remember, many senior citizens, students and the unemployed cannot afford to buy tickets at full price.

Even if the group is not trying to make money, think twice before making it a free event (unless performing in a space where it is difficult to take money, like street theatre). Audiences do not attach a value to free shows. They do not feel they have to turn up. Simply charging £1 makes people feel they are committed to the show.

P for Promotion – how to sell the show: Like the secret of good comedy, timing is the most important tool in promoting a show. There are a number of tried and tested ways to market a show, ranging from the expensive to the free. Whatever your group decides to do, make it creative and have fun.

TIMING

This is a suggested plan for marketing. Do not be put off if you have less time, it can all be condensed into a few (very busy) weeks. Consider marketing your group's show using some or all of the tools listed below. It may seem obvious, but do not plan to have posters printed before the venue is confirmed and do not ask the cast to distribute leaflets during their dress rehearsal.

Producing print: Up to six months before the show, start to think about leaflets and posters (print). If the group has not done this before, approach printers to find out costs as soon as possible. Decide how many leaflets and posters will be needed, based on all the other planned marketing. Remember that the more print produced, the less the price per item. Also remember that the size of each will determine cost. Postcard-size leaflets will be cheaper than A4-size leaflets, but might not be suitable if a lot of information has to be included.

Think about the number of colours required and the quality of the paper. A simple photocopied leaflet on coloured paper may be enough. A full-colour poster will be more eye-catching but more expensive. A compromise is using just two colours – for example, a black-and-white photograph with the title and copy (the writing) in bright green. Think about how colours look together. Black and red seem like a good idea for *The Dracula Spectacular* but black type on a

How long before first night	What to do
One year to go	Start looking for a sponsor
Six months to go	Find a printer
	Choose or design an image
Three months to go	Print posters and leaflets
	Start to build up a press list
	Design a web site
Two months to go	Send out a press release
	Distribute posters and leaflets
	Write a letter to your group's mailing list – offering priority booking period
Six weeks to go	Call the press contacts with ideas for stories
	Get the adverts designed
	Start to design the programme
One month to go	Start advertising
	Get the programme printed
Two weeks to go	Check ticket sales. 'Firefight' if necessary
One week to go	Call the press to make sure they are coming to the press night
On the night	Pamper the sponsors and the press
	Hand out questionnaires and marketing list forms
	Start to think about the next show

dark red background is difficult to read, particularly for visually impaired people.

Find out how long the printer needs to produce the print. Decide when to start distributing it and work backwards to give yourself enough time. Make sure the printer sticks to his/her commitment to get the print to you on time. Ask for all information – timing, quantities and costs – in writing, just in case anything goes wrong. Also find out how many proofs you will see and how many times changes or corrections can be made.

Some information is so important it should always appear on the print. Check that your posters and leaflets contain the following:

- the dates, time and days the show is on
- the range of ticket prices (including concessions, which are usually shown in brackets)
- the title of the play and the author
- the name of the group performing
- where the show is being performed
- how to get tickets
- your web site address
- a few lines about the show or the group
- any other details which are required by the show's copyright owner or venue management

Make a list and ask lots of people to proof the print for spelling and missing information. Do not rush the proofing. Even professional theatres sometimes forget to include the box-office phone number and wonder why no one buys tickets!

Probably the most important decision about the print is what artwork or image your group wants to use. The image can give the potential audience a good idea of what the show will be like or it can be something eye-catching and unusual that intrigues people. The group could create its own image, either by taking photographs or asking someone in the group to draw an illustration or create a computer graphic. Check that your group's design does not infringe anyone else's intellectual property, which, as well as copyright, includes trademarks. Check your local bookshop for royalty-free graphic books. Some clip art may also be reproduced free of charge. If in doubt, always ask permission.

However, if the director's heart is set on an existing image, the group may need to obtain permission to use it if the image is protected by copyright or is a registered trademark (often denoted with the '®' symbol). This means some detective work to find the original illustrator or the organisation which holds the rights to the image. It will almost certainly cost money to use the image. The cost will often depend on the number of posters and leaflets being produced.

Press coverage: Press coverage is free, apart from the time dedicated to making it happen and the tickets and hospitality given to members of the press when they come to your show. Many professional theatres have a dedicated press office that deals only with this side of marketing because it is so important. About two months before the show goes on, write a press release and send it to all the local papers. Make it as short and catchy as you can – no more than one page. Perhaps use an attention-grabbing device. One group in Scotland performing Brian Friel's *Lovers* sent out a packet of Love Heart sweets with each press release to get it noticed. Use a headline that will attract attention, then set out the facts. Remember that journalists will (hopefully) use your copy to write the article. Include information about the group, the show, the cast, when and where it's on, when the press night is and whom to contact for more information. If possible, give a daytime phone number.

If your group is known locally, include details of the last production. If it is a one-off show or a new group, tell the journalist why you are putting on this show now. These snippets of information should be interesting enough to make the papers want to find out more. Think about who the press release should go to. Who came along to your last show? Check details of previous reviews. Phone round the local papers to find out who deals with the arts. There is no point sending a press release if the journalist has no interest in the field.

Another way to get a show noticed by the papers is to arrange to take publicity photographs in strange and picturesque places. If performing *The Importance of Being Earnest*, dress up your Lady Bracknell and ask the local bag shop if you can organise a photo with her choosing a bag. Most businesses will be happy to agree in return for some free publicity and will be very accommodating.

There is no point sending a press release if the journalist has no interest in the field.

The group can also organise competitions with tickets as prizes. The great thing about this type of marketing is that your group can normally organise them at quite short notice so you don't need to give away seats you might have sold. Simple competitions are great for local newspapers as it increases their circulation if readers know they can win things by buying the paper.

The Internet: Ask the Internet experts in your company to create a web site for your group or the show. Do your own gimmick web site or simply a site with details of the show, the actors and reviews of past shows. Rules for Internet advertising are similar to more traditional methods of advertising, and include the British Codes of Advertising and Sales Promotion (as referred to below). Advertise the site on your print and tell the press about it so they can get information. Give an e-mail address so people can respond, or reserve tickets.

A good web site will be kept up to date, which encourages surfers to keep in contact and visit the site regularly. It may be possible to form a databank of links to other sites, some of which may be happy to reciprocate with a link on their site back to your group's web pages.

Tell people not to give their credit-card or debit-card details to the group over the Internet unless the site has secure encryption technology and you have the facility for credit-card authorisation. If not, surfers can check ticket availability on a regularly updated web site and reserve seats to be paid for later. The Consumer Protection (Distance Selling) Regulations were introduced in October 2000 to strengthen a consumer's rights when purchasing goods or services via the Internet, as well as by mail order, telephone or fax. However, booking various leisure services, including theatre tickets, is excluded from the Regulations, and therefore tickets may still be sold on a no-returns basis. Other services, including costume hire, are covered by the Regulations, and any group wishing to undertake these types of transactions should obtain legal advice first.

Distributing posters and leaflets: Once the posters and leaflets are printed, there are lots of ways to get them to potential audiences.

Many towns have a professional distribution company who manage racks in pubs, restaurants, leisure centres and colleges. The cheapest way is to get the cast and the whole group to take leaflets and posters around town and persuade local businesses to display them. Bookshops are good sites especially if your play is an adaptation of a book. They might create a big display if you agree to run a competition to win tickets for the opening night. If your group is performing a musical, ask the local music shops to do the same. Ask your chairperson to write to these companies, and perhaps enclose a couple of tickets to say thank you for their cooperation. Local libraries and community halls may also be willing to display posters.

Fly-posting is an offence under the Town and Country Planning Act, 1990, and may additionally create ill feeling. Posters under A3, displayed no more than twenty-eight days before the show (and removed within fourteen days of the last night of the show), are normally acceptable, but always contact the local authority's planning department. The person putting up the poster, the landowner and the group may all be subject to enforcement proceedings if an offence is found to have been committed.

Posters or banners on or near public highways are tightly controlled by the highway authority. Under the Highways Act, 1980, a group can be fined up to £2,500 per poster if consent is not obtained.

Additionally, any landowner who has not granted permission can seek repayment for the costs of removing any unauthorised posters, and for any other damage caused to his or her property.

Letters to a marketing list: Marketing lists are the most cost-effective way of encouraging people to buy tickets. You are writing to people who have already expressed an interest in what the group does. However, this method of marketing requires a lot of time and effort. It may not be suitable if you are a new group or are producing a one-off show. It may be possible to ask other groups to send out details to people on their mailing lists, especially if the arrangement is reciprocal.

It may not be practical to collect names and addresses when people are buying their tickets, particularly if the tickets are sold by the local school, shops or sports centre. There are other ways, like handing out a form to everyone who comes to see the show and asking them to fill it in and hand it back before the end of the night. In return, your group might offer priority booking periods or money off the ticket price for early bookings. There are lots of ways to encourage loyalty and make the people on your mailing list feel special.

The Data Protection Act, 1998, states that if your group wants to collect and use names, addresses and other details, you have to ask that person if s/he wants to go on your group's marketing list. More details about the Data Protection Act are on pages 230-3.

Advertising: This is certainly an expensive marketing tool, but it can also be the most effective at encouraging a new audience to attend. Advertising also reminds the loyal audience that they still have time to book. As with print, the number and size of your adverts will be dictated by the budget, as well as where you want to advertise. Advertising prices are usually quoted per column centimetre (pcc). Alternatively, ask for the cost for a quarter-page or an eighth-page, which may be cheaper. Ask for a written quotation which shows the size of the advert and the dates it will appear for the group's records. It is likely that once placed, an order cannot be cancelled or refunds made.

Consider advertising in the free local papers or other more unusual outlets, including local transport (backs of buses) or billboards. Joint projects with local businesses might allow a cost-effective multi-channel advertising campaign.

Programmes: Once audience members have paid and have arrived at the venue, it is often a good idea to give them more information about the show, in the form of a programme. These can range from a full-colour booklet with lots of advertising and articles about the show to a photocopied list of the cast. Do not waste money on programmes. The group might be able to sell a glossy booklet but it takes a lot of time and effort to produce. It may be better to produce something quick and easy, which you can give away on the night.

MISLEADING ADVERTISEMENTS

Overall, the publicity material should be checked to make sure it does not mislead. An audience member who purchases a ticket relying on statements made in publicity material may be disappointed if those statements are not realised, and may even have a claim for damages against the group. If publicity is designed in such a way as to deceive the public into thinking they are attending a show produced by a different group, that other group may have a claim for the profit it has lost by the diversion of ticket sales under the rules of passing off.

The Trade Descriptions Act, 1968, makes it a criminal offence to knowingly or recklessly make false statements about services or facilities. The Consumer Protection Act, 1987, makes it a criminal offence to give misleading information about prices of services. The Director-General of Fair Trading may, in addition, consider complaints about misleading advertisements and apply to the courts for an injunction to prevent them.

THE BRITISH CODES OF ADVERTISING AND SALES PROMOTION

The Committee of Advertising Practice and the Advertising Standards Authority (ASA) are responsible for the self-regulatory system that deals with complaints about non-broadcast advertisements. They publish a code of practice and offer a complaints-handling process for anyone who feels that the codes have been broken. Ultimately, under the Control of Misleading Advertisements Regulations, 1988 (amended in 2000), if an advertiser does not remove an advertisement that the ASA has ruled against, it may be found to be in contempt of court.

The codes set down a number of principles which are applied in the spirit as well as the letter of the codes. They include the principle that all advertisements:

- must be legal, decent, honest and truthful
- should be prepared with a sense of responsibility to consumers and to society
- should respect the principle of fair competition
- should not bring advertising into disrepute

Your group should have evidence to back up any claims made by your group (for example, 'biggest festival in the world'). Obvious exaggerations which are unlikely to mislead may be acceptable, since people readily accept that adverts often contain a level of 'hype' or 'spin'. Special care should be taken if an advert makes comparisons to other shows. If so, the comparison must be objective and must not create confusion.

The advert should not contain anything which would cause serious or widespread offence and should comply with legal requirements. It is the advertiser who has primary responsibility to comply with all relevant regulations. The Committee of Advertising Practice provides advice pre-publication to advertisers, and publishes general and specific guidance on its web site.

In addition to the voluntary codes, various specific statutes contain regulations controlling advertisements. Many rules only apply to specific goods and services, but some operate to protect consumers generally.

FIRE-FIGHTING

It is worth having a couple of ideas just in case all the marketing has not done enough to get the audiences into the venue. There are two possible issues at stake if there is no audience. The first is whether or not the group has sufficient resources to continue. The second is whether or not the audience is big enough to make the venue look busy.

If your audience is simply not big enough, the best thing to do is 'paper the house' (give away tickets to people who you know will turn up). This can be achieved through local community centres or charities, ticket give-aways in the local paper or simply walking the streets and persuading people to come along. Be careful of giving away tickets in case people do not turn up. Concentrate on those people you think will talk about the show once they have seen it. Whatever you do, try to fill up the opening night (especially if you have members of the press reviewing the show or sponsors who want to see how successful it has been). Word of mouth is the best and the cheapest marketing tool there is.

RESEARCH AND MONITORING

If your group is planning to produce another show in the future, the best way to save money is to consider what marketing worked and what did not. Ask the audience (perhaps using a printed questionnaire) where they have come from, did they enjoy the show and most importantly from the marketing point of view, why they attended. Did they see the advert in the paper, did they see a poster, pick up a leaflet, read a review or is it simply that someone told them about the show? Knowing all this, and counting how many people were influenced by which marketing tool will help you to target the marketing next time.

Health and Safety

INTRODUCTION

Performance venues are full of potentially dangerous situations, equipment and materials. The *Stage* has reported several deaths in 2000 of professional backstage crew. These accidents happen despite a comprehensive and complex framework of health and safety legislation. Although some of these regulations may not apply to the voluntary sector, most do, and it is advisable for all groups to be aware of these rules. A breach of the regulations may give rise to a criminal prosecution, and could lead to a claim for personal injury or even corporate manslaughter.

Whether a group hires or owns its performance space, it owes a duty to its members, governing body and audience to provide a safe environment in which to enjoy the show. Performing arts activities are classed as 'work activity' and are therefore subject to the Health and Safety at Work Act, 1974. Different duties exist for employers and owners of venues, but generally check to provide:

- safe equipment
- safe systems of work
- information, instruction, training and supervision to ensure safety
- safe buildings, and safe means of access to and exit from the building
- risk assessments to identify which measures are required to comply with health and safety law

The Health and Safety at Work Act, together with its raft of supplementary regulations, contains most of the current legal framework.

The latest regulations are contained in the Management of Health and Safety at Work Regulations, 1999, and a code of practice was published in March 2000. Other regulations are set out in the Factories Act, 1961, and the Occupiers' Liability Acts, 1957 and 1985, or in Scotland, the Occupiers' Liability (Scotland) Act, 1960, as well as many other specific regulations. Some regulations only apply to some parts of the country. In general, the emphasis of the statutory framework is to take reasonable precautions. Failure to do so may lead to claims for compensation from anyone who has been injured, criminal prosecution and a local authority cancelling a theatre licence.

> An accident involving a veteran musical comedy artist happened during a summer show at the Westcliff Theatre in Essex. The artist was wheeled in a wheelchair on to the stage by a comedian. The comedian misjudged the distance to the edge of the stage, the wheels of the wheelchair caught the edge and the artist was tipped into the orchestra pit, sustaining serious injuries.
>
> ABTT Update, March 2001

HEALTH AND SAFETY AT WORK LEGISLATION

It is important to realise that although the main thrust of the Act is to protect employees, it also applies to other areas. It covers:

- non-employee workers
- volunteers, contractors and members of the public
- self-employed people
- non-domestic premises used by visitors

Even if your group does not employ anyone and only rents its performing space, your landlord will have to comply with the rules, as will any contractors you use. Other duties of care arise when a group hires equipment to other people, or organises fund-raising events such as sponsored walks or swims. Therefore, take health and safety regulations into consideration. Reasonable steps must be taken to provide and maintain an environment which is safe, without risks to health and with adequate facilities for welfare at work. The practical problems and cost of safety arrangements are taken into consideration when deciding what is 'reasonably practicable', but each decision by a court or tribunal will depend upon the facts of each case.

Employees must take reasonable care of their own safety and of the safety of others. Everyone, whether an employee or not, must not interfere with health and safety measures, such as blocking fire escapes or damaging fire-fighting equipment.

HEALTH AND SAFETY POLICIES

A written health and safety policy is mandatory for all employers with five or more employees. Other groups would be strongly advised to create a policy, which demonstrates the group's commitment to a safe environment. Most policies start with a general statement, reaffirming the group's commitment to addressing safety concerns and then sets out who will be responsible for meeting those concerns. Finally, the policy will set out the practice and procedures for each identified risk. The Health and Safety Executive (HSE) publishes examples.

Once drafted, the policy should be checked regularly, to see if it remains up to date, or whether any specific activity needs to be addressed.

It is likely that any policy will contain a framework for identifying risks and how to assess its impact. This is especially important for a drama group, because each show is likely to have a number of different health and safety issues. All employers are now under a duty to produce a risk assessment (in writing if there are more than four employees). For each show, consider completing a risk assessment which:

- identifies potential hazards (machinery, set, special effects, etc.)
- identifies who is at risk (performer, crew, audience)

- estimates the risk factor (taking into consideration the severity of injury and the likelihood of the event occurring)
- states precautions that should be taken to avoid the risk or combat the risk at source
- estimates the residual risk after taking those precautions

If the employee is under eighteen years old, the employer must carry out a specific risk assessment, to take into account that person's lack of experience or awareness of risk. Consider giving information to a child's carers to make sure that they are fully aware of both the risks and the preventative measures taken. Particular attention should also be given to expectant and new mothers and their babies.

Although a risk assessment takes time, it avoids a group becoming overfamiliar with the risks of live performance and also helps to highlight new areas of concern. Show conditions can be stressful and people can behave differently when they feel under pressure. Take this into account in a risk assessment. If the residual risk is still high, consider taking further action, perhaps by preparing a health and safety scheme to help put a plan into action to deal with these residual risks. Specific guidance for the control of substances hazardous to health (COSHH) is available from the HSE.

Also remember that it is not just the acting space which must comply with health and safety legislation. Each area of the venue, including auditorium, front-of-house, orchestra pit, corridors and dressing rooms, present their own risks. Some West End shows, such as *The Witches of Eastwick,* contain special effects which take place over the audience. Other shows involve the entrance and exit of actors through the auditorium. Dressing rooms contain flammable materials, including costumes, wigs and make-up. It is also tempting for actors to use dressing rooms as a smoking area. This combination is potentially dangerous.

REGISTRATION

Groups with no paid staff will not need to register with either the HSE or the Environmental Health Service Department (which is part of a local council). However, the entertainment licence procedures include health and safety aspects, and especially dangerous events, like firework displays, will require registration.

EMERGENCIES

Procedures should be in place to deal with emergencies before they happen. Everyone involved with the show should be aware of these procedures. Make sure that your group knows how to deal with the following basic procedures:

- **Medical emergencies**: Immediately notify front-of-house manager or stage manager who will contact the emergency services if required.
- **Fire emergencies**: Be aware of the location of fire-fighting equipment. If a fire is suspected or discovered, immediately notify the front-of-house manager or stage manager. Sound the nearest alarm. Leave the building, closing all doors.
- **Power failures**: If possible, turn off appliances to prevent damage when power is restored. It may be necessary to evacuate the building. Take care because the exit route may be darker than usual.
- **Bomb threats**: Treat all threats seriously. Immediately notify the front-of-house manager or stage manager. The respective manager will decide whether it is necessary to evacuate the building.
- **Evacuations**: Make sure everyone is familiar with the emergency procedures, especially the exit routes from the building. If there is time, close doors and windows, notify other people in the immediate area, and leave the building using the nearest safe exit. Report to the front-of-house manager or stage manager. Do not go back into the building until instructed it is safe.

DUTIES OF THOSE RESPONSIBLE FOR PREMISES

If the group is responsible for premises, it will be under a statutory duty to take reasonable care to make sure that the property is safe. It must also take reasonable steps to make sure that entrances and exits, equipment and materials are safe. The statutory duty has been extended to ensure that occupiers of premises must avoid risks of injury to anyone, with no distinction between those who entered with or without permission. Remember the rules apply to all of the building, not just the stage and auditorium, so that dressing rooms, loading bays, kitchens and storerooms must also comply.

To summarise these duties (the list is not comprehensive):

- **Health**: Provide adequate ventilation, a reasonable temperature, suitable lighting and keep the space clean.
- **Safety**: Keep the premises in a good state of repair and any machinery in good working order. Make sure there is enough space to move easily. Doors, windows, floors and stairs should all be safe. Proper equipment should be made available, especially if working overhead. Helmets and gloves may be required.
- **Welfare**: Provide well-lit, ventilated and clean toilets and washing facilities. Theatre licences normally contain a minimum number of toilets for males and females. Provide drinking water. Define areas for smokers and non-smokers.
- **Fire safety**: All premises must comply with fire-precaution regulations, and premises which are accessible by the public must have a fire certificate. Precautions include the provision of fire extinguishers, fire exits and fireproofing scenery, props and drapes. See Stage Management on pages 159–1 for more details. Regular fire drills should take place. The Fire authority enforce and monitor fire safety, and are consulted before a theatre licence is granted. The local fire brigade can advise on appropriate fire alarm and prevention systems. New safety sign regulations are in force, which must be followed to clearly mark fire exits. There is now an EU-approved logo for emergency exits. Signs stating 'No Exit' must not be

used, because they are easily confused in emergencies. Use 'No Entry' instead. Special consideration will be given to ensure the safety of people with mobility difficulties.

- **Seating**: Detailed rules are in force, including the number and minimum width of gangways, minimum distance between stage and audience, and between rows. Seats in each row must be fixed together in groups of at least four. Each seat also has minimum standards (area and construction). Special rules exist for promenade performances (or standing areas in an otherwise seated auditorium) and cabaret-style venues with loose chairs and tables. The capacity of the venue will be agreed as part of the public performance or theatre licence and must not be exceeded.
- **Electrical appliances**: All equipment must comply with the Electricity at Work Regulations, 1989. Cables must be in proper order and must be out of reach of the public. Luminaires must be securely fixed with a safety chain. Lifts must be properly maintained and inspected every six months.
- **Manual handling**: Some sets, props and equipment may be heavy and require moving in less than ideal conditions. Provide information to backstage crew to minimise the risk of injury.
- **First aid**: Theatre licences are normally conditional on providing a defined level of first aid. Consider making sure that there is at least someone suitable on duty to provide first aid for performances, and at all other times, that a fully stocked first-aid box is available.
- **Food hygiene**: This is a special area of health and safety regulation which applies to any group that prepares, supplies or sells food. The group must supply food and drink that is safe to consume. It may be necessary for those responsible for catering to attend a basic food and hygiene certificate course. Seek detailed information from the environmental health department of the relevant local authority.
- **Trade waste**: You may be under a duty to keep waste secure so that it does not escape and to dispose of your waste safely and legally.

SECURITY

To ensure the safety of your members and audience, consider taking the following precautions:

- Keep your cash float to a minimum. Keep the float in a cash register or other lockable money box. Two people should move excess cash to a secure place. Do not leave money at a venue overnight. Bank all takings, preferably taking an escort, and varying the time and route.
- Do not leave personal property unattended. Lock storerooms and dressing rooms when not in use. Lock all vehicles and do not leave vehicles unattended while unloading.
- Use some form of identification, to keep out strangers. Issue passes and politely challenge anyone who does not have a pass. Use door attendants and keep a list of who should have access to the backstage areas. Consider issuing a uniform for front-of-house attendants – which may be as simple as a customised T-shirt.
- If anything is stolen, report it to the local police station immediately. Use 999 only in emergencies.

KEEPING RECORDS AND REPORTING ACCIDENTS

Keep records of all emergencies and ensure that next of kin, senior management and insurers are informed. Employers must have an accident book, which must be kept for at least three years. Some accidents have to be reported under the Reporting of Injuries, Diseases and Dangerous Occurrences Regulations, 1995 (RIDDOR). These include a death or major injury, an over-three-day injury (that is when an employee or self-employed person has an accident at work and is unable to work for over three days, but does not have a major injury), a work-related disease, and anything else that happens which although not resulting in a reportable injury, clearly could have done. From 1 April 2001, all reports will be processed by the Incident Contact Centre in Caerphilly.

Stage Management

The Theatres Trust has condemned Britain's historic venues as restrictive, dangerous and in serious need of major improvement.

Stage, 14 December 2000

INTRODUCTION

Some groups are lucky to have access to state-of-the-art performance spaces. Most will be subject to the patch-and-repair policies that many venues have been forced to adopt. Other sections of this handbook highlight the people who are likely to be in charge of the performance space and the general health and safety issues. However, this section draws together some of the key issues relating to stage work. The performance space will always be the hub of your group's activities. It is dynamic in nature, not only changing in character from show to show, but also from scene to scene. For most people who perform, the stage will not be a very familiar space, which makes its inherent dangers unexpected.

The art of stage management is good planning. Someone should be in charge, someone who should work closely with the director throughout the planning and rehearsal process to ensure that by the time the production reaches the performance space, as much as possible has been ironed out. The planning process must include some allowance for the unforeseen, but the stage manager is likely to follow a timetable which includes:

- strike and get-out – removing a previous set from the performing space

- rigging – installing the lighting required for the performance
- get-in and fit-up – set construction
- focusing and plotting – making sure the lights are positioned correctly, and that the lighting and sound levels are recorded for each different setting for the show
- props and wardrobe – adding furniture, props and set dressing to the set, and distributing costumes backstage
- technical rehearsal (the tech) – rehearsing the show to check that all the elements referred to above work well together on stage
- dress rehearsal – a final run-through of the show (without stops)
- opening night

The risk of injury continues throughout the run and it is important that no one becomes complacent. Stage management may consider creating a show report for each performance which could include notes of anything that did not go to plan. Any problems, however small, should be reported to the stage manager who can deal with the situation before it turns into a crisis.

THE SET

Some acting areas have audience on all four sides (in the round), with actors making entrances via the aisles between the seating. Here, any set has to be carefully placed to ensure that the actors can be seen by the audience. Special consideration is often given to the flooring to create the right atmosphere. Open, or thrust, stages have audience on three sides. The back wall can be used for scenery and entrances. Traditional, or proscenium, stages tend to be raised, with the audience directly in front. Promenade performances (where the actors move from area to area, with their audience following) tend to rely on a smaller amount of set, making use of the natural surroundings. More details are included in the Open-Air Performances in Part 1. More recently, there has been a growth in installation theatre, where the audience moves through an area which has been especially designed for a particular event.

A set must therefore fit on to the area available and be suitable for the position of the audience. The show may have particular demands and many scripts include a suggested floor plan showing the type of set required. A director may also want the action to take place in a particular setting or period, which will also impact on the set.

If a group makes or buys its own sets, it will need somewhere to construct and store the scenery. Premises can be borrowed, leased or purchased. All reasonable steps must be taken to ensure that the premises, entrances, equipment and materials are safe and free of risk to health.

Parts of a set are likely to be large and heavy. Some may be required to move into position with some speed. Others may have to be electrically wired to produce an effect. All of these factors mean that the set can potentially cause personal injury. Stage hands and performers should be introduced to the set, and any special risks pointed out.

Most sets are built of wood, cloths, gauzes and drapes. These materials are naturally flammable. Although the fire safety officer responsible for each venue will know what is acceptable at that venue, as a general rule all scenery should be made flame-retardant. Plastic and polystyrene will need special consideration. Some stage furnishings and props may also require flame-proofing, especially if naked flames appear on stage. Note that some chemical treatments used to increase flame-retardancy can cause irritation to skin.

Depending on the resources of the group, sets can be purchased, hired or made. Making scenery for the professional stage is a specialism, and a group may need help if a set has to cope with flying or touring.

PYROTECHNICS AND OTHER SPECIAL EFFECTS

If naked flames or pyrotechnics are required in the show, it is important to liaise as soon as possible with the local fire officer and the local authority health and safety officer. They may wish to visit the performance space to approve installation and operation for each special effect to ensure that the public are not in danger. If there could be a danger to crew or cast, expect the officer to disallow its use. Suitable precautions will include the following:

- use material designed for the stage – never be tempted to invent your own pyrotechnics
- read the instructions, and install following the manufacturer's guidance. The operator should always be able to see the special effect to make sure that it is safe
- real flames (if allowed at all) should be kept away from combustible materials. A fire officer may need to supervise the ignition of a flame used on stage, and will remain in sight of the flame until extinguished
- candle holders or ashtrays should be sturdy, and if possible fixed in position. You may be required to partly fill an ashtray with wet sand
- storage arrangements should be checked – it may be necessary to have a locked storage space, with special labels, to avoid any naked flames or smoking near to highly flammable materials

MOTOR VEHICLES ON STAGE

Driving a car or similar on to a stage can produce a spectacular effect, but the presence of a combustion engine creates risks. Check to see if alternatives can be used effectively – can the vehicle be pushed, an electric motor be used or set constructed to accommodate a stationary car? If not:

- drain the fuel tank to the minimum needed for each performance and lock the fuel cap
- plan for exhaust fumes
- make arrangements for the filling of the tank and storage of spare fuel
- keep a drip tray under the vehicle when not in use

Never be tempted to invent your own pyrotechnics.

SMOKE MACHINES

Smoke effects are produced by dry-ice machines or smoke guns. The former warms up frozen carbon dioxide to produce the smoke effect. The frozen blocks need careful handling. Carbon dioxide is heavier than air, so its use may be restricted if there is not sufficient ventilation – especially if the performance space has basements or an orchestra pit. More modern smoke canisters produce a non-toxic smoke effect. However, they still need to be operated carefully to ensure that they do not produce so much smoke that the audience cannot see the stage or the fire exits.

LASERS AND STROBOSCOPE LIGHTING

Lasers are potentially lethal, so they are tightly regulated. The Health and Safety Executive has published a British Standard for laser specifications. All laser equipment should be installed, maintained and operated by professionals. They will make sure the siting of the laser (and associated mirrors) will not harm the audience.

Strobe lighting which flashes more than five times per second can produce epileptic seizures. Short exposure to strobe effects may be possible, especially if other lights are used. Warning notices must be displayed at the main entrance to the venue to warn the audience of the use of strobe effects.

FLYING

Moving scenery using ropes, pulleys and weights can be risky. Moving actors in a similar way for special 'flight' sequences requires special skills. Use an expert and special flying harnesses.

FIGHT SCENES

It is easy for an inexperienced performer to accidentally cause injury to another actor during a fight sequence. Use an experienced fight choreographer and keep the stage as clear as possible. Work in good light, wearing non-slip shoes on non-slip flooring, using weapons with blunt points and non-slip handles. The actors should always keep a safe distance, and perform the fight at a sensible speed. Consider if it would be possible for the actors to wear gloves and eye protectors. Always rehearse using the stage weapon, so that an actor does not need to adjust to a weapon of a different weight, and allow time for actors to warm-up and rehearse the fight before each and every performance.

PROPS

Some scripts have prop lists printed at the back. This may be a good starting point, but do not rely on it. Check the script carefully with the director. A few props will be required for rehearsals, but it may be possible to use a 'stand-in' before the show. Some of these will need to be 'practical' or 'functional', for example a telephone may need to ring. Other props will need to be replaced after each performance. These props, often called 'comestibles', include cigarettes, food and props that are (intentionally) broken. All food should be prepared in hygienic surroundings, covered and refrigerated until required. Alcohol should not be consumed in large quantities (if at all) on stage. Non-alcoholic alternatives exist.

Using money on stage can cause problems. Notes need to look convincing without being a forgery. A cheap alternative is to use real foreign currency.

The props should be stored safely. Small items are often laid out on a table with a space marked for each prop, so that it is easy to spot any missing items. Actors often like to look after their own personal props, and it may be necessary to track down a prop or two that is misplaced during the run. It should go without saying that a very close eye should be kept on valuable or dangerous props.

FIREARMS AND OTHER WEAPONS

It should come as no surprise that the possession of guns is tightly controlled. The Firearms Act, 1968, applies to all guns and ammunition. The controls contained in the Act were extended in 1996 following the Dunblane tragedy. It is a criminal offence to possess or purchase a firearm without a police certificate. A firearm which has been deactivated, checked and stamped by a government-approved professional, so that it cannot fire live or blank ammunition, does not require a certificate because, in effect, it is no longer a firearm. The deactivated weapon should still be kept securely, and you must advise the local police of its presence at the venue in advance, in case it is mistaken for a real gun.

A certificate will be required for other firearms, including, in most circumstances, replica guns that only fire blanks, if they could be converted to fire live ammunition. The certificate will be issued to the producer or other person responsible for the performance by the police authority for the area in which the applicant lives. The certificate will be granted with strict limits on the type and number of firearms and ammunition.

Most sports starting pistols and other replicas or toy guns not capable of firing live ammunition do not require a certificate, but local rules or regulations may exist. These types of pistol are designed to fire blanks at arm's length, with the barrel pointing up, and they may be dangerous if fired in any other way. Even starting pistols are noisy, to the point of potentially causing damage to a person's hearing, and emit a dangerous discharge which could cause personal injury. No firearm should be pointed at the audience or directly at an actor. Aiming slightly to one side will have the same visual effect and lessens the risk of the actor being hit with any discharge from the firearm.

All certificates contain a condition that the firearm or weapon must be kept safe and secure when not in use. Blank ammunition must be limited to the amount required for the run of the show, with only the amount needed for each performance removed from a locked store. Never use or store live ammunition. The person named on the licence must be present at all times when the weapon is not locked in storage. Only that person can carry the firearm in public. However, the actor does not need a certificate for possession of the firearm or weapon on stage for the performance.

There are companies which are authorised by the Home Secretary to supply weapons for shows, and they will be able to provide more information about a particular gun. Further advice is also available from the police force firearms licensing department which deals with the venue. If in doubt, find an alternative, like a toy gun or a pre-recorded sound effect.

Knives, swords and other offensive weapons (including some martial arts weapons) are controlled by the Criminal Justice Act, 1988. It is an offence for anyone to carry these in a public place unless they are used for work, religious purposes or part of a national costume. The stage is not a public place, but rather a working area, and so no actor breaches the Act if s/he carries a weapon. However, the Act may be breached if that actor walks through the audience to reach the stage, or carries the weapon during publicity events outside the venue. As a precaution, contact your local police force for advice.

These props raise health and safety issues, and should be subject to a specific risk assessment exercise. Actors must be trained in their use and all potentially dangerous props should only be given to the cast member on their way to the stage and taken to safe storage immediately after the actor has left the stage. These props must not be left unattended. Firearms, ammunition and other weapons must be locked away between performances, and any loss must be reported immediately to the police. Do not take any chances: even blanks can kill.

WIGS AND COSTUMES

Some groups design and make their own costumes, particularly if the show is set in modern times. Others, especially those staging pantomimes or musicals, may hire the whole wardrobe from one of the costume-hire firms. Resources normally dictate which route to follow.

Impersonation of a police officer is a criminal offence. However, uniforms are allowed in the course of a performance of a stage play at a licensed theatre as long as their use does not bring them into contempt. The same exception does not apply during publicity or photo shoots or other activities outside the venue. As well as uniforms for police officers, the following uniforms are also controlled:

* naval
* military
* air forces
* uniformed chartered associations (such as the Girl Guides)

MAKE-UP

The choices available to make-up artists have increased in recent years. Traditional greasepaint can be combined with other types of foundation, rouges and lipstick, etc., to achieve (with practice) professional results. Latex is useful in the right hands, but be careful with the adhesives that are used to keep the latex in place. Always read the instructions and test on a small area of skin for adverse reactions. Latex and adhesive allergies are common. Be extra careful of make-up near the eyes: those members not used to eyeliner may need some extra help. The HSE has produced a booklet which includes guidance on the health risks associated with exposure to natural latex.

COPYRIGHT

It is not just the playscript that has copyright protection. Any plans or drawings of scenery, costume or make-up designs are also likely to enjoy the same protection. This means that it is not possible to copy someone else's plans without their permission. However, there is no copyright in a particular idea: the famous black-and-white Ascot scene from *My Fair Lady* is one idea of a way to present that scene. The idea can be reused, but it would not be possible to copy the dresses without infringing the designer's rights in the detailed costume sketches.

A recent claim by the original make-up designer of *Cats* for breach of copyright illustrates the point. Every time the make-up is applied, it is a copy of the original make-up design. The designs cannot be used without permission.

Nothing stops costume designers using designs as a source of inspiration, to create their own new designs. Some design books state clearly that any design can be used to make costumes, without paying a royalty to the original designer.

If the group uses a consultant to design a set or costume, make sure the terms on which the design can be used are clear, and if possible in writing, for the group's records.

BORROWING

This must be the cheapest way of getting what is needed. It may take a little longer, but a little detective work (and lots of delegation) can work.

- Give some background on the group, the show and the specific item to be borrowed.
- Be clear on the available budget, and if no fee is available, offer advertising in the programme, or free tickets.
- Provide insurance cover details.

- Mention other people if they have allowed you to borrow items.
- If this enquiry is not successful, ask for any other suggestions to stop the trail going cold.
- Never borrow anything of sentimental value as no amount of insurance proceeds can replace it.
- Think twice before borrowing anything of high value, because your insurance cover will have an upper limit.
- Keep written details of the lender and the borrowed item. Issue a receipt. Agree a date (and method) for return.

HIRING

Some items would be too expensive to make or purchase, or too specialised to borrow. Hiring can provide the answer. A leasing or hire agreement is a contract between the owner and the borrower regulating the terms on which the item is lent. Most of the large hire companies have pre-printed order forms which include detailed terms and conditions. If you are not familiar with these terms and conditions, ask for a copy before placing the order. Check the terms carefully. Seek clarification if needed. Most terms are not written in stone and it may be possible to negotiate better terms. If so, the alterations may need to be in writing and signed by the hire company.

Even if there are no written terms, there will probably be a binding legal agreement. Keep notes of any telephone conversations or meetings during which important issues were discussed or agreed:

- Do you know the terms and conditions of the hire contract?
- Will the hired goods need special use, care or handling? If so, is training required?
- If there are specific requirements, let the lender know. Make sure the requirements are understood and form part of the contract – the small print may try to exclude the lender's responsibility for failure to take account of specific requirements, so make sure any promise is in writing and signed by the lender.

- Check the hired goods all arrive in a good condition. If not, inform the lender immediately.
- Check arrangements for collection or delivery.
- Check storage arrangements.
- Return the goods in the same condition. If alterations are required, seek permission first.
- Return the goods on time.
- Insure the goods.

Sound Effects and Music

Some venues are so large that it will be impossible for the actor to be heard by the whole audience without amplification. In other situations, it may be necessary to balance the voice of one actor against other sounds that occur at the same time. The same sound system may also be used to create atmospheric sound effects or to play recorded music.

USING MICROPHONES

Microphones can be fixed in position and connected to a sound control board by leads. Alternatively, radio microphones can be used, which transmit signals to the sound board without the need for wires. In either situation, the sound generated on stage will need to be balanced to maintain some uniformity. Radio microphones must operate on approved frequencies, to avoid interference with the emergency services or taxi firms.

SOUND EFFECTS

Most sound effects in the professional theatre are pre-recorded on to tape or digitally on to CD, DAT or mini disc. Creating your own sound effects can be a hugely enjoyable challenge. The alternative is to use someone else's recorded sound effect. The BBC, for example, has created a series of recordings which are available from music shops or may be stocked by your local library.

Radio microphones can interfere with the emergency services or taxi firms.

MAKING A COPY OF EXISTING RECORDINGS

Copying someone else's recording is subject to the rules of copyright. If you wish to copy an existing sound recording (even if it is to transfer the recording from one medium – for example, a tape recording or computer file – to another – CD) you must obtain permission if the recording is protected by copyright. Most copyright owners use the Mechanical Copyright Protection Society to authorise the copying of a protected work. .

PUBLIC PERFORMANCE OF A RECORDING

Playing a recording in public is also restricted by the copyright rules. Almost all record companies only permit a sound recording to be played in private. If you want to play a recording in public, you will need to obtain permission. Phonographic Performance Limited (PPL) administers licences on behalf of copyright owners. PPL normally grants annual or 'one-off' licences to venues. The venue operator may require you to keep records of which recordings were played, so that an annual return can be made to PPL of all recordings used during that year.

PUBLIC PERFORMANCE OF ALL MUSICAL WORKS

The copyright in a musical work is separate to the copyright in any recording of it. Whereas the PPL issues licences for the recording, the Performing Rights Society licenses public performances of live or recorded musical works. This includes music used as an overture, entr'acte or exit music and other incidental music played to an audience before, during or after a show. It also includes music that is performed by a character on stage, or is audible to a character. A licence would therefore be needed from the PRS if a character sings a song or plays a record in the course of a play's action. This is known as 'interpolated music'. The PRS does not control performance of full musical works, such as musicals and pantomimes (known as dramatico-musical works), or musical works specially written for a play when performed during that production. In these cases, or if the composer is not a member of the PRS, it is necessary to obtain the composer's consent. Remember that any lyricist and any arranger may have a separate copyright to the composer. Copyright for a musical work expires seventy years after the end of the year in which the composer died.

The PRS normally grants annual licences to venues. In addition, it requires at least thirty days' notice for interpolated music. Both the venue owner and your group could be liable for payment of royalties. If in doubt, check with the PRS theatres officer.

It is worth restating that for the public performance of recorded music, permission must be sought from the PPL for the use of the recording and from the copyright owner (or the PRS on the owner's behalf) to perform a musical work in public. This is because there are separate copyrights in the recording and in the musical.

RECORDING A PERFORMANCE

Permission to make a recording of a performance will be required from the copyright owner (or the Mechanical Copyright Protection Society if it looks after that owner's rights). This applies not only to sound recordings but also to video recordings. A different scale of rates is payable to professional musicians if their work is recorded.

SPECIAL RULES FOR SCHOOLS, COLLEGES AND PLACES OF WORSHIP

No permission to perform a copyright musical work by pupils or teachers is needed if it takes place during school activities in front of an audience of teachers and pupils only. If parents are present, the normal procedures above will apply, because this will be classed as a public performance. Educational establishments should contact the Centre for Education Management for further details.

Performances during religious services in places of worship do not require a PRS licence.

AVOIDING NOISE POLLUTION

Excessive noise can become a nuisance and it can be dangerous. There is evidence that prolonged exposure to high levels of noise can cause hearing loss. Very loud noises of shorter duration (like gun shots) can also cause problems. Sound levels should therefore be carefully checked as part of a health and safety review. This will ensure that the noise created will be safe for the audience, performer, backstage crew and musician.

Some venues are in close proximity to residential areas. It is likely that the venue's theatre or public entertainment licence will contain conditions on the level of noise that can be heard from outside the building. If in doubt, your local environmental health officer from the local council may be able to provide guidance.

Front-of-House

'Front-of-house' describes the multitude of activities that take place in direct contact with the public. It is now widely acknowledged that the front-of-house area and the personnel have a large impact on the audience. Even the smallest performing space will need a well-managed auditorium to ensure the public feel comfortable and safe. Venues usually have spaces such as the foyer that are open to the public during the day. People may use these spaces to check details of shows, book tickets or buy refreshments. Venue owners grant visitors an implied permission to use these free access spaces, but this permission can be revoked at any time and for any reason.

Manchester's Royal Exchange Theatre is a steel-and-glass structure constructed inside the old Exchange building. During the day, the theatre is cordoned off and no permission is granted to visitors of the building to enter that space. However, the venue managers positively encourage visitors to enjoy its many other facilities. A few minutes before a performance is due to start, front-of-house staff ask all visitors who do not have tickets for the show to leave the building to make sure the audience and actors are not disturbed.

THE BOX OFFICE

This may be the first contact that a member of the public makes with your group. First impressions do count, and a badly run box office will lead to disappointed audience members. It is also important to ensure that the box office is managed well because it is responsible for handling a large percentage (if not all) of the group's income. If this goes wrong, it could lead to financial embarrassment for the group. Box-office staff, or the treasurer or ticket secretary, will need financial and marketing skills:

> The Alexandra Theatre in Birmingham is offering free admission to the first 10 nuns to turn up to a sing-along version of *The Sound of Music* on 3 April. Staff have been ordered to keep their eyes out for impostors.
>
> *Guardian*, 11 March 2001

If the group uses a professional theatre, it is likely to use a modern, computerised box-office system, which may also be accessible via the Internet. The group may be offered box-office facilities as part of their arrangement with the venue. However, it is likely that the venue managers will wish to recoup some of the costs of operating the box office by charging a commission. If your group chooses to use the venue's box office, it may be possible to arrange to sell tickets jointly – so that those sold by the group directly to its membership and contacts do not trigger a commission payment to the venue.

Decide before any tickets are sold whether any particular warnings or information should be given about the content or staging of a show. Some shows contain material that is not suitable for children. Others may include special effects which could cause distress to some people. More information may be required if your venue is not normally used as a theatre, to make sure the audience can find the venue and know where to park.

Also consider setting aside a number of tickets for each per-formance to cover emergencies. These are often called 'house seats'. They are left empty until the last moment, just in case there are any problems. House seats are normally located in an easily accessible part of the auditorium. If seating is not numbered in a particular venue, then 'reserved' signs might be placed on those seats. Also set aside any tickets which will be used for publicity – either for press reviewers or sponsors. These are often the best available seats in the house. However, every ticket given away may be a seat which could have raised direct revenue for the group. For small theatres, there is often a delicate balance between the benefits of a newspaper review and the benefits of receiving cash from a paying audience member.

The next group of tickets might be reserved for any 'patrons', 'friends' or other subscription scheme. It may be possible to encourage a loyal following by keeping an appropriate allocation available. For all mail-order purchases:

- Open the post and record the date each item was received.
- Keep all of the contents of each letter together – order, payment and any SAE.
- Review each order. Make sure the cost of the order is covered by the amount of the payment. If any part of the order is not clear, make notes on it to refer to later if need be.
- If any problem cannot be resolved (no payment or no tickets left, for example), contact the sender. It may be that they would be prepared to accept a different priced ticket or tickets for a different performance.
- Check the payment (is the cheque signed and dated?) and make sure the payment can be traced to a particular order – this is important if the cheque is returned by the group's bank as unpaid.
- Allocate tickets.
- If possible, a second person should check the total payments received against the total value of tickets sold. These two figures should balance before any payments are banked or tickets dispatched, to catch any mistakes.
- Dispatch tickets (or arrange for them to be collected) and bank the payments.
- Consider whether each purchaser's details should be added to the group's database for future marketing.

For telephone sales, the professional theatres have arrangements with credit-card issuers to accept payment, even though the customer is not present at the box office in person. These arrangements, also called 'merchant' agreements, can be expensive. The alternatives are:

- accept reservations by telephone, and 'hold' the requested seats for a set

number of days to allow payment to be received
- to operate an information service, so that customers can check ticket availability

GROUP SALES

Most organisers positively welcome group bookings – it is seen as a quick way to fill the venue. However, group sales are not without their own problems. If an enquiry is received, it may be worth checking with the person making the booking that the show is suitable for those attending – some shows may not be suitable for all groups. It may also be worth setting out the details of the booking in writing – the risk of getting the booking wrong is less if it is checked and double-checked by the person making the booking. Also make clear whether any special terms apply to the ticket sales – it may be worth considering an extended time before payment is due or group discounts or free teacher tickets.

REPORTING

If tickets are issued to cast or crew to try to sell to friends and family, record the number of tickets given to each person. Insist that payment is received or the tickets returned by a set date. This will avoid confusion and embarrassment later.

For each type of ticket (free/discount/full price) keep a list of the number sold (and at what price, if there is more than one) for each performance. Not only will this provide an invaluable reference for accounting purposes (especially if the group is obliged to pay a royalty to the author of the show), but the group may be able to spot important trends well before first night.

TICKETS

A person who has paid to see a show has a legally binding agreement with the seller, regardless of whether or not a ticket is issued. However, a ticket provides 'proof' that the agreement exists, and may help indicate any special terms and conditions on which the ticket was sold. A group could print its own tickets using the templates available in some computer desktop publishing packages. Alternatively, it could use cloakroom-style tickets, as a cheap pre-printed alternative. If the seating is more complicated, or security is an issue, the group should consider ordering tickets from a specialist printer.

The information on the ticket is very important. The following information might appear on the front or back of a ticket:

venue
name of show
group name
date and time of performance
refund/exchange policy
'Latecomers will not be admitted until a suitable break'
'The management reserves the right to refuse admission'
'Photography and recording devices are strictly prohibited'
'The venue operates a no-smoking policy'

Always check with the author or the author's agent, the venue and the public licensing authority to see if any particular statements must be printed on the tickets.

Note that if the customer does not see these statements until after the ticket has been purchased – for instance, if the ticket was purchased by telephone – it may be difficult to prove the statements form part of the binding terms and conditions of sale. Similarly, a statement printed in the programme will probably not form part of the agreement with the customer since it is only available after the sale of the ticket.

A performance may have to be cancelled, shortened or changed, and it is worth spending some time considering what the group would do in these circumstances. At law, your group made a promise to provide a service (to admit the audience member into the auditorium to see a show) in return for the ticket price. If the show is cancelled, your group may be in breach of its promise depending on the terms of the translation. If in breach, the purchaser of the ticket is entitled to some form of redress. In most cases, any difficulty can be overcome by the offer of a ticket for another performance, but the purchaser of a ticket may be entitled at least to a refund of the ticket price, and perhaps other costs which reasonably follow the cancellation of the performance, depending on how reasonably foreseeable these costs might be. Obvious grey areas exist, especially where the show is cancelled part-way through. To avoid doubt, make sure the group has a refunds policy which is brought to the notice of the purchaser before the ticket is purchased.

Before 1999, there was no general duty to make refunds to anyone who was not the ticket purchaser. Under the Contracts (Rights of Third Parties) Act, it is likely that anyone who holds a ticket may make a claim, regardless of whether they purchased the ticket or were given the ticket as a present.

THE FOYER

A front-of-house manager may take responsibility for this area. The house manager may need to coordinate a number of ushers – either paid or volunteer workers who assist in selling programmes and refreshments or directing audience members to their seats. The minimum number of attendants is often set by the health and safety requirements for the building. This number should be observed at all times and for each performance. This may be difficult, with some volunteers only able to assist for some of the performances. Each attendant should be given some basic training in safety issues, and some background to the building, seating arrangements and the show. They will also need to know what to do with latecomers, or people who have lost their tickets.

Cloakrooms: One of the first concerns for the visitor may be whether a coat or bag can be left with an attendant during the show. If an attendant accepts any article for safekeeping, that person assumes a duty of care irrespective of whether a charge is made for the service. The venue management will ordinarily be responsible for the acts of its attendants. The exact level of care will depend on a number of factors, depending on what is reasonable in the particular circumstances. At the time the item is accepted, reasonable limits on liability for loss or damage to the item must be made very clear on a receipt, ticket or notice. These disclaimers should not be contradicted by any verbal statement made by the attendant, which could render the limitation completely ineffective.

Some venues provide a coat rack, without any attendants. If the venue has not accepted responsibility for articles left on the rack, and has not taken possession of them, it will probably not be held responsible for any subsequent loss suffered by the owner. This should be carefully balanced against any ill feeling that may be felt by someone who has had their item stolen.

All theatre licences will state the minimum number of toilets that should be provided at a venue. Health and safety officers may also be able to provide further guidance.

Refreshments: Any sale of alcoholic drink will require a licence, and will need to comply with the weights and measures regulations. Your group will have a responsibility to ensure customers are served proper measures. These rules are enforced by the local trading standards officers. Health and safety should be paramount for all sales of food and drink.

Displays: It is common to display photographs from the current production and details of forthcoming attractions. All displays should be carefully situated to make sure they are not dangerous and do not block fire-escape routes.

THE AUDITORIUM

A ticket holder has the right to occupy the allotted seat to view the show so long as s/he conducts him/herself properly and complies with any conditions imposed when purchasing the ticket. Proper behaviour is measured with due regard to the other audience members. An audience member should not stop the performance – if s/he does not like the show, s/he should leave quietly.

If someone's behaviour is unacceptable – for example, by being intoxicated or by taking prohibited photographs – the venue management may be entitled to require the person concerned to leave. The reason for the request should always be given. The person should be allowed time to leave, but if s/he does not go, they can be treated (in England and Wales) as a trespasser. It is legitimate to use reasonable force to make sure a trespasser leaves. If in doubt, or if more serious disorder occurs, call the police.

Dealing with unruly audience members is not the only concern. There will normally be rules set down by the venue's management which your group will have to comply with, including regulations addressing public licensing or other safety concerns. These may include a 'no standing in the aisles' rule, or a 'no glasses in the auditorium' rule.

LOST PROPERTY

If an attendant finds lost property, the venue managers should look after the article until it is reclaimed. If an audience member finds lost property, the finder will have the right to possession. This right continues until the owner claims the article. Either way, reasonable steps should be taken to find the proper owner, which could include reporting the loss to the police. After making reasonable enquiries, the property can be sold if not reclaimed by the owner within a reasonable time. If a finder does not take reasonable steps to find the owner, then the finder could be guilty of theft. A special procedure for valuable property is set out in the Torts (Interference with Goods) Act, 1977, or the Civic Government (Scotland) Act, 1982. It is an offence not to comply with these obligations.

OUTSIDE THE VENUE

If queues form – for tickets or to enter the venue, or for any other reason – it is the responsibility of the venue managers to control the crowd to prevent them becoming a nuisance to neighbours. Although the police do not have a primary responsibility to supervise queues, they should be consulted to avoid breaches of the peace.

The venue may have access to parking facilities, and much like the guidance given above to cloakrooms, the terms on which a patron uses the car park should be clear.

More relevant to neighbours will be the level of noise or other disruption suffered, especially at the end of a performance. This nuisance will have been considered when the local authority granted a theatre or public entertainment licence, but there will always be a measure of compromise. A discreet reminder to patrons, especially if the venue is in a residential area, may be worthwhile. Unreasonable disturbance could lead to legal proceedings or complaints to the relevant local authority, who could refuse to renew a licence or, in some situations, could revoke an existing licence.

Accessibility

INTRODUCTION - WHAT IS 'ACCESS'?

Since the late 1990s, the importance and promotion of access, or 'Arts for Everyone', has rapidly become one of the key priorities in all areas of arts policy. So what is meant by 'access'? The most common usage of the term relates to buildings or public spaces and the access which they do, or do not, permit. If there are steps, rather than ramps or lifts, then 'access' for people using wheelchairs is severely limited. Access, however, goes far beyond physical architecture. If a venue is located at the end of a poorly lit back street in an area known as a local trouble spot, some members may not feel comfortable using that building. A venue situated in the suburbs of a town or city might suit car owners or local residents. If it is not well served by public transport, then those living outside the immediate area without a car or money for a taxi will, in turn, find access to this space problematic. Even with the ideal location, the group's membership, or its audience, may not be a representative cross-section of the local population. Some sections of the community may be involved in a group's work while other sectors could be under-represented.

A recent controversy over white actors blacking up in an amateur production of *Showboat* highlighted this issue. The group argued that they were open to members of all racial backgrounds; that they could not be held responsible for the fact that there were no black members within the group; that *Showboat* was a piece which contested racial segregation and was evidence of their best political intentions. Leaving aside the particular issues of the practice of blacking up, the key question in relation to the access debate is why had this group,

Accessibility: what if the building is in an area known as a trouble spot?

existing in a multicultural area of Britain, been unable to recruit black actors to play black roles in this production in the first place?

Many groups may identify with the problems faced by this particular group and be able to identify similar problems with their own membership profile. Perhaps the group is dominated by women and finds men difficult to recruit; or there is an absence of younger people; or the group is predominantly from the professional classes or one particular ethnic background.

THE DISCRIMINATION DEBATE

The day-to-day decision-making processes of your group will, by necessity, involve some hard choices. Your decisions may mean that some people get what they want and some are disappointed. The audition process is a good example of a situation which compels your group to take some form of action, which, by definition, discriminates one actor from another. No one would argue that, in the considered opinion of the casting committee, and everything else being equal, the best actor should not be offered the part. It is accepted that the criterion for the decision-making process – the ability of the actor – is fit and proper, and can be morally justified. No one likes to lose, or feel excluded, and this is a perfectly natural response. We are all social beings, and being told that someone's skills or opinions have been valued more highly than one's own can be hurtful. However, as members of society, we accept that decision as long as the process or competition was fair.

If the process was unfair, or unequal, the aggrieved individual may justifiably feel that their skills or opinions have not been given proper consideration. Developing mechanisms to make sure that all of your group's processes are fair will help ensure that your members, potential members and audiences will not feel alienated, ignored or abused.

EQUAL OPPORTUNITIES

Some people are discriminated against (sometimes on purpose, sometimes unintentionally) for reasons that cannot be justified. In some areas, laws have been brought into effect to stop these types of injustice. The Sex Discrimination Act, 1975, states that it is illegal to discriminate because of a person's sex and (in employment situations) because of their marital status. The Race Relations Act, 1976, makes it illegal to discriminate because of a person's race, skin colour, ethnic origin or nationality. Only limited exceptions apply where a particular sex or race is a genuine requirement for a job to maintain privacy and decency. For employers, it is now illegal to discriminate on the basis of gender reassignment.

The need to protect children and other vulnerable members of society overrules the normal anti-discrimination rules relating to ex-offenders. See pages 109–10 for the new rules relating to access to criminal records.

New measures were introduced by the Disability Discrimination Act in 1995 to help combat discrimination against disabled people. These new rules apply to all who provide services to the public. Public performances will therefore be subject to the Act. Your group must not discriminate against a disabled person by treating that person less favourably than another person for a reason connected to a disability, or, alternatively, must not refuse to make reasonable adjustments to the way that the service is delivered. The Act defines disability as a physical or mental impairment that has a substantial adverse effect on a person's ability to carry out normal day-to-day activities, where this effect has lasted or is expected to last for at least twelve months. It is already contrary to the Act to refuse to provide a disabled person with a service, provide a lower standard of service, or provide a service on worse terms. This means that your group might have to provide clearer signage at a venue for visually impaired members of the audience or an induction loop system for people with hearing difficulties. From 2004, reasonable adjustments to premises will also be required to overcome barriers to access.

However, there will be situations where you may not have to make such adjustments, for instance, if the adjustment requires major changes which would fundamentally affect the nature of your group's work, or if the cost of altering the premises is prohibitive. Each challenge brought before the courts will be judged on its own merits, so it may not be legally necessary, for example, to install a lift for wheelchairs if another entrance is available or a ramp has been fitted. There is no legal reason to provide wheelchair access to the circle if space is made available in the stalls. Guidance on the meaning of 'reasonable' adjustments is available from the Disability Rights Commission.

In relation to discrimination on the grounds of religious belief, the Human Rights Act, 1998, grants individuals the right to freedom of thought, conscience and religion. Although the Act does not have a direct impact on non-state organisations, it may become a standard that all groups will aim for. Similarly, age discrimination and discrimination on the grounds of sexual orientation are increasingly becoming the subject of voluntary codes of conduct which may become enshrined in legislation soon.

THE BENEFITS OF INCREASING ACCESSIBILITY

It is well documented that participation in arts activity increases self-awareness, self-confidence and self-motivation. The performing arts also promote communication and social skills, cooperation with others, and the self-belief that comes from direct acceptance by a group and its audience. These are the key benefits available to all who participate in the performing arts, and they can be seen as vital to those who may have particular needs in these areas. Participation may lead to a much greater quality of life for those involved. Moreover, the improvements to any individual's quality of life will always have a direct and positive effect on the communities in which the individual lives and works.

Widening access can also benefit the current membership by increasing their awareness of the needs of others. Prejudices against those communities seen as 'other' to one's own can be confronted and challenged by working creatively with individuals from sections of society which the current membership might otherwise never encounter.

Also, a new member from another community, suburb, occupation, ethnic background or generation to existing members will enlarge the existing audience and increase the group's revenue. The increased audience figures will also result in an improved profile which will help the group's reputation and increase the chances of securing funding from public bodies in the future.

A group which consists of predominantly one gender, or people from a particular class, ethnic background or generation will necessarily restrict the type of production it is able to produce. Increased access makes more appropriate casting possible, thus eliminating the need for actors to play other genders or ages, or the need to represent those from races different to the actor's own. People from diverse backgrounds bring diverse readings to any piece of work and a rich diversity within the group will reap its own rewards in enriching that group's approach to its process and production.

HOW TO INCREASE ACCESSIBILITY

It may be worth stating categorically the grounds on which decisions are made:

> No member shall be discriminated against on any grounds other than (during the audition process) talent and ability. Any person who feels that he or she has been unfairly discriminated against may raise the issue with [the chair of the group].

If the ideal location for auditions, rehearsals or performances is not available or affordable, other solutions can be implemented. Could there be a 'pick-up point' where people can access lifts from car-driving group members? Is there enough money in the group's funds to pay taxi fares home? Could a minibus be laid on to transport audience members to the production? Solutions like these may already be informally practised within your group, but publicise them in your recruitment and marketing material.

The venue's name, common usage or cultural location can hold associations which may implicitly restrict access. Theatre spaces themselves are far from neutral; most come with a particular cultural and economic history which appeals to already established clientele. Looking for alternative venues to show your work might make the same show accessible to a much wider audience.

These problems with access are among the most complex that your group will address and there are no easy solutions to them. Once a group has established itself as predominantly of one ethnic background it becomes very difficult to open the group up to individuals from outside that ethnic community. Similar problems may be experienced across social classes and backgrounds or between generations. Where there is a majority membership that can be perceived as 'other' to the individual who is considering joining the group, there may be an access problem. Careful choice of venue can eliminate the more obvious examples of exclusion outlined above by avoiding places of political, religious or ethnic affiliation. Try strategies such as using a neutral meeting place as the initial contact location. This can help to diminish the impact of the nature of the rehearsal space itself, giving people a chance to meet representatives of the group on neutral ground first. Your group's commitment to their participation can be communicated in person, countering any potentially negative first impressions.

The major obstacles which will restrict access to your group are not physical obstacles but people's perceptions of what your group is and whom your work is for. That is why your group's choice of show, and your marketing and recruitment strategies, are crucial to the success of any access-widening initiative. Before addressing the way your work is marketed, you need to address the nature of your group's work, and how broad a cross-section of the public can be expected to engage with the subject material. To demonstrate a real commitment to access, people of all ages, backgrounds and cultural communities should be given equal input and opportunity to contribute to the work and not have their contribution restricted to playing a minor role or stereotype which they, and the community they come from, are likely to find patronising and offensive.

There is no lack of diverse work available, yet the same plays are produced over and over again. Encourage key members of your group to read around before play-choosing time, to discover new scripts which offer possibilities for greater diversity within the cast. A good source for new material is the web site www.opentheatre.co.uk/cpad/ which has a database of over 300 previously produced community plays. Alternatively, create your own script, or adapt an existing one (subject to copyright restrictions). This is often the ideal way to ensure that a diverse membership has equal access to the work produced and does not need to be as intimidating as it may at first appear. General advice for employers is available from the government under their advice and information service, Equality Direct.

OUTREACH

If your group's marketing is only targeted at friends, families and contacts of existing group members, then you are restricting future access to your group to members of those communities already represented within it. Marketing through local papers or library noticeboards can be useful but will not, in itself, indicate to potential members whether the work will be appropriate for them. In addition to generalised marketing, you must prioritise the new communities you are wishing to access and target them accordingly with posters or flyers.

There may be individuals from other generations/communities/ cultures who could be persuaded to join the management committee of the group even if they have no interest in becoming directly involved in a show. They will then be in an ideal position to recruit from their own communities, helping to develop a wider accessibility to the group's work. Any potential member will then perceive the group as one which already has representation from their particular community and so feel more confident that the group will be appropriate for them. In addition, a greater diversity of representation on your committee will provide a more rounded view of your group's provision. Members will be able to advise where they see potential problems for access which might not have occurred to someone from outside that particular community.

A collaborative project with another group is an ideal way to widen accessibility to the work of both groups – for that particular project and in the future. A joint project between an older group and a youth group, or between an Asian group and an Afro-Caribbean group, will bring double audiences to the joint project, so introducing both audiences to the work of the group they have had no former access to. Many of these new audience members may return to future work of the partner group, or even wish to participate in future productions. Diverse communities often bring diverse skills and performance traditions with them and co-productions are an ideal way of widening the scope of your group's work. The future profile of each group will also appear less selective and more accessible.

As an alternative to a full-blown collaboration you may want to consider contacting a wide diversity of communities through groups already in existence, and offering them one-off workshops, or a series of drama sessions led by existing members of your group. If your members are prepared to visit different communities in their own cultural centres or youth clubs, they will have the opportunity to introduce your group and its work to a much wider range of people than would ever be motivated to attend an audition on the strength of an advert. If this kind of work is undertaken prior to holding auditions, you will already have made the first contact with prospective members and hopefully gained their interest and support on 'home' territory, enabling them to feel more confident about their right to access your group's work wherever that might take place.

Once you have decided on appropriate subject material and put into practice your strategies for recruitment, the next stage is to examine the audition process itself. While for some groups, selection is inevitable and necessary, it is worthwhile checking to make sure that your selection process is not loaded in favour of existing group members, working against any widening of your current group profile.

MONITORING AND EVALUATION

The best way to identify issues that are of specific concern to your group is to monitor, and then evaluate, who is able to access your work at each stage of the production:

- To find out your current membership profile, ask all members to fill in a form setting out age ranges, sex, ethnic origin, employment status, postcode and space for a description of any disability. As long as the identity of the individual cannot be ascertained from the form, there is no data protection issue.
- At the audition, ask all new members to fill in a form like the one above. Other useful questions to add to this form would be: How did you hear about the audition? Why did you decide to attend the audition? How did you find the audition? Is there anything which caused you problems?
- Keep a record of those who are selected and mark whether they are new or previous members.
- Keep another record, if necessary, of those who were selected but turned down the part. Try to identify and record their reason.
- Keep a register of attendance. Make a note of those members who drop out during the process and, if possible, their reason for dropping out.
- Ask each member of the audience to fill out a form just like the original membership form but with the addition of the following questions: How did you hear about the production? What made you attend the production? How did you find the production?

Remember that collecting information from named individuals is subject to the Data Protection Act, 1998. Some of the data referred to above is classed as 'sensitive' and will require each individual's express consent before it can be used. Special regulations permit using sensitive information for equal-opportunity monitoring, as long as there are sufficient safeguards. The Commission for Racial Equality is expected to publish guidance.

Having kept these records you will now be in a position to evaluate your group's current membership profile. If you feel your efforts to increase access are not working, you will be able to see precisely where the problems are. You can now draw up an informed action plan for the next production you undertake, and decide which points of access you are going to prioritise and which communities you would like to see better represented in your group.

This might all seem like yet another burden of work which nobody really has time to do, and monitoring and evaluation systems are time-consuming processes. However, this time is well spent if your group can then identify which marketing and recruitment strategies are working and which are having no effect; which areas of the city, or which communities are worth putting more time and effort into, and which are simply not going to be interested in your group's work. Knowledge like this can save time, effort and money, and make your administration and publicity workload run much more efficiently and effectively. In addition, monitoring and evaluation are procedures which funders are increasingly requesting, so in addition to sharpening your own practice you will also be increasing your chances of securing additional funds for your work.

3 Management

Amateur Theatre Groups

Performing groups fall into two categories: those groups specially formed to present live performance, and those which exist for other reasons but would like to produce a show as an entertainment, educational or fund-raising exercise. This section introduces the different group structures, the methods of decision-making, and the rights and responsibilities of the members of these groups. It contains sample clauses of a governing document which are illustrative only and may not be suitable for your group's particular situation. Getting the structure right for your organisation will help to clarify roles, duties and potential liabilities of the group and its members.

TYPES OF ORGANISATION

The way an amateur theatre group is organised affects the activities of its members, and how the members relate to each other within the group structure. It also has important legal and financial consequences.

Sometimes it is possible to choose which structure will apply to your group and therefore which set of special rules will apply. To try and simplify a very difficult area of law, this section assumes that the group is a not-for-profit organisation. This means that at the end of each period, the group's income (after paying expenses) is retained by the group or distributed to other not-for-profit groups, rather than paid to its members. In other words, members do not pay their subscription fee in the hope of obtaining a good financial return!

Legally, there are only a small number of possible structures for not-for-profit organisations:

- unincorporated associations
- companies limited by guarantee
- trusts
- industrial and provident societies
- friendly societies

A new form of legal entity, the limited liability partnership, has been available since 1 April 2001. At the time of writing, whether it will be suitable for amateur theatre is hard to predict, but guidance published by the Department of Trade and Industry presumes that limited liability partnerships will operate for profit.

By far the most popular types of structure for amateur theatre groups are unincorporated associations and companies limited by guarantee. Either of these types of structure can be set up for charitable purposes, and so it is possible for a group to be:

- an unincorporated association and a charity
- an unincorporated association but not charitable
- a company limited by guarantee and a charity
- a company limited by guarantee but not charitable

Unfortunately, the name given to the group will not necessarily indicate the type of structure that the group has adopted. A group calling itself a 'Theatre Company' may be an unincorporated association or a company limited by guarantee.

UNINCORPORATED ASSOCIATIONS

An unincorporated association is an association of persons bound together by identifiable rules and having an identifiable membership. This common intention creates the organisation, rather than any formal registration process. If a group is not part of another organisation, is not a trust, limited company, friendly society, nor an industrial and provident society, and is not incorporated under royal charter or statute then it will be, by default, an unincorporated association. Many societies and clubs are unincorporated associations.

This type of organisation is quick and cheap to set up, and has a flexible structure. However, these associations are not legally recognised as a body separate from its membership. This means that liability rests with the association's governing body or, in some cases, its members. Liability to third parties is not limited by the structure. Whoever is found to be responsible for a liability may be forced to use his or her personal assets to meet that liability. For further details see the section on liability of members and officers on pages 234-6. It also means that any property must be held by some of the members on behalf of the other members. This type of structure is therefore less suitable if the group is entering into risky agreements, or enters into long-term arrangements including employment contracts. It is also less suitable if the group owns land and property, which may need to be formally transferred to other members if the original named owners leave the group.

All associations must have rules (also known as its constitution), although the rules do not have to be written. If they are not recorded, then there is opportunity for uncertainty. The founding members should agree on the rules which will form the constitution. Model rules are available from umbrella organisations or solicitors to provide some framework for this discussion. Once agreed, the founding members should formally adopt the constitution, agreeing to abide by those rules, by holding a meeting and either signing the rule book or the minutes of the meeting as a record of their agreement to the constitution. See page 207 for more details about constitutions.

COMPANIES LIMITED BY GUARANTEE

There are two types of limited liability company: those limited by the value of the issued share capital (owned by members who purchase shares in return for a proportion of the company's profits) and those limited by the amount of guarantees given by its members. The latter type does not have shareholders, but rather members who promise to contribute a sum (normally less than £10) if the company becomes insolvent. The limit to liability is fundamental to the limited company and protects the members from losses larger than their agreed contribution. The principle of limited liability does not apply in all situations. Members of the governing body may be personally liable if they act fraudulently, negligently, outside their powers or otherwise contrary to statute. The benefits of limited liability come at a cost. The main disadvantage is the formality and quantity of the related paperwork. The documentation required to set up a limited company is fairly complicated and copies must be sent (together with a statutory declaration and a formation fee) to the central registry, known as Companies House. The records at Companies House include details of the finances of each registered company and details of each director, including the director's home address. All these details are accessible by the public. However, some funding bodies prefer to work with companies because of this transparency or public accountability.

A limited company can own land and other property and defend any legal proceedings in its own name. It exists in its own right as an organisation which is different to its members. It will continue regardless of how many members come and go. It is therefore popular with groups that own land and buildings or employ staff, or enter into other long-term arrangements.

To start a company limited by guarantee, the founding members must complete various forms required by Companies House. The company must have a rule book, and the Companies Act, 1985, sets out a standard version, sometimes referred to as 'Table C'. A company's rule book is known as its 'memorandum and articles of association'. The statutory default may contain provisions that do not work in your group's particular circumstances, but it is possible to adopt a different rule book or amend the standard version as long as the alterations comply with the Act.

Once all the documents have been gathered together and sent to Companies House with the formation fee, the Registrar of

Companies will issue a certificate, which will show the company's name and its unique company number. This process normally takes a week or so. Specialist company formation agents exist who can help with the formation process, but a solicitor may be able to provide a wider range of advice.

OTHER TYPES OF STRUCTURE

A trust is an arrangement created when one person or organisation transfers property to a group of people called trustees. They own that property on behalf of a defined group of people. Trusts are normally set up by a formal document (the trust deed), which will record the rules under which the trust will operate and the obligations of the trustees. A trust is not a membership organisation; instead trustees have strict duties to act in the best interests of the trust and its beneficiaries (Trustee Act 2000). This type of relationship is known as 'fiduciary'. Trusts are often used for grant-making bodies, and in England and Wales, the duties of trustees are automatically assumed when land is owned by more than one person.

Industrial and provident societies are benevolent cooperatives set up to provide life assurance or other benefits or services to their members or the wider community. It is unlikely that this has ever been an attractive structure for amateur theatre groups. Since 1993, only mutual assurance societies have been able to register as friendly societies.

If your group exists for some other purpose, it may still have one of the structures set out above. Alternatively, it could be part of a different type of organisation, like a school or a church. If your group is part of a larger group, it may be that your governing body is a subcommittee of the larger group. The subcommittee should be clear as to whether it has authority to make decisions and how it reports back to the main group.

CHARITIES

All not-for-profit organisations (regardless of their structure) can be charitable. If all of the group's aims and objectives are charitable, it will be a charity. Drama groups may be charitable if their objects are seen to advance education or are beneficial to the community by promoting the arts. Fund-raising itself is not a charitable purpose, but only a mechanism to allow an organisation to fund its activities which may be charitable. In England and Wales, charitable associations, companies or trusts must register with the Charity Commission, unless they fall within the small charities exemption: income less than £1,000 per year, no interest in land or other permanent endowment (Charities Act). If the exemption applies, or the group is in Scotland, registration is not required, but the group should be recognised as a charity by the Inland Revenue.

Charities enjoy tax advantages (see page 250-61), and a charitable organisation may find that some funding is available to it which is not available to non-charitable groups. However, charities are tightly regulated, including restrictions on trading. A charitable drama group selling tickets for a show is not viewed as trading, because this relates to a service which is being provided by the charity as part of its educational charitable work. Ancillary trading activity may be allowed (such as selling refreshments to audiences during intervals), but running a costume-hire business will be classed as trading. Although a charity cannot trade, it can set up a separate subsidiary trading company which will be controlled by the charity through its governing body.

Because there is a potential conflict of interest between the charity and its governing body, special rules exist which restrict payments to committee members. No remuneration can be paid to a committee member in return for their services as a committee member. However, if a committee member is also, for example, a professional set designer who wishes to charge the group for her design services, then this can take place if:

- the governing document allows reasonable payments to be made to committee members
- the rest of the committee (with the person concerned not being present) decides that the price payable is fair for the work, and that the payment will not put the charity's finances at risk
- (in England and Wales) permission is granted by the Charity Commissioners

All charities must have a written constitution and must prepare annual accounts which are open to public scrutiny. The Charity Commission publishes model constitutions for groups wishing to register as charities. Some umbrella organisations also supply models which have already been approved by the Commission. The constitution is formally adopted by the group and a copy sent to the Commission for registration. If a charity in England or Wales has an annual income or expenditure of over £10,000, it must prepare an annual report for the Charity Commission and, in any event, should produce accounts. Land transactions follow a special procedure. The Inland Revenue and the Charity Commission both publish comprehensive guidance.

Members of the governing body of a charity, because of the fiduciary relationship, will be personally liable for the charity's losses if they act in breach of their duties. See pages 234-6 for more details.

If some of the group's activities are not charitable, it may be necessary to separate the charitable activities from the non-charitable activities to ensure that the group maintains its charitable status. This could mean that your group may consist of two organisations: a charitable organisation and a trading organisation.

NAMING THE ORGANISATION

Choosing the group's name is likely to have long-lasting consequences. Consider using a name that relates to the group's current role, but also one which can cope with changes in the future.

Sheffield boasts a number of amateur operatic societies, including Sheffield Teachers' Operatic Society and Manor Operatic Society. The first was formed by members of a particular profession, the second after a particular geographic region of Sheffield. Both are long established (the former for over 100 years) and now encourage membership from a much wider base. However, their only limits are those set down in their respective rule books.

Before settling on a name, check to see if it is used by another organisation. If there is a danger that two organisations could be confused, there is a risk that your group could be forced to stop using its name and potentially be required to pay damages to the existing organisation. If the group wishes to have a presence on the World Wide Web, it will need a domain name address. The more logical the domain name is, the better chance a surfer will have of guessing it. Using the initials of the group's name may be an alternative if the name is too long or already in use. Remember that in general web names are allocated on a first come, first served basis.

Subject to the above, and except for a few prohibited words ('Limited', 'Girl Guides', 'British Legion', for example), an unincorporated association can adopt nearly any name it wishes. Stricter rules exist for names of companies. A registered company's name cannot be the same as an existing company name and should not be too similar to an existing name. Offensive, sensitive, misleading or controlled wording cannot be used. Companies House produces detailed guidance. A company must use the word 'limited' (or Welsh equivalent) in its name, but companies limited by guarantee can apply for an exemption to this rule.

A company can always use a trading name in addition to its registered name. Any name other than the full registered name is a trading name. An abbreviated trading name might be useful for publicity, but the full registered name must be used on company stationery (probably including web sites and e-mails), bank accounts and contracts (Business Names Act 1985). For example, 'AD Theatre Co' could be the trading name for the Amateur Drama Theatre Company Limited.

Registered charitable organisations have their names recorded by the Charity Commission or, in Scotland, by the charities division of the Inland Revenue. Any abbreviated names must also be recorded. The name will be rejected if it is the same as, or similar to, an existing charity's name, or is misleading or offensive. The Charity Commission publishes detailed guidance.

Although the group's name does not attract copyright protection, any logo, symbol or other design which represents the group's name may be protected by copyright. It may also be possible to register a name or logo as a trademark or service mark, although trademark registration is likely to cost hundreds of pounds.

THE GOVERNING DOCUMENT

After choosing a structure and a name, it will be necessary to set down the rules under which the group will operate. These rules, or constitution, should make it clear who can become a member and how decisions are made. They may take the form of a written constitution or a company's articles of association, but are collectively often referred to as the 'governing document'. It is likely to include provisions dealing with:

- the group's name (and perhaps location)
- the group's objects (or purpose for which it has been created)
- any express powers that are required to allow the group to undertake any activity (such as the power to purchase land and buildings)
- any express restrictions on the activities of the group – especially if the group is charitable (such as a prohibition on political campaigning)
- the rules relating to membership (who can join, subscription fees, etc.)
- the rules relating to the board of directors or committee members
- the rules relating to members' meetings (how often, voting, etc.)
- record-keeping, accounts and audit
- how to alter the governing document
- how to dissolve the group

Other formalities may be required on adopting a constitution under company legislation or charity law. For example, companies are under a statutory duty to provide a copy of its memorandum and articles to anyone who requests sight of them. To make the processes of decision-making as clear as possible to your membership, provide your group's members with a copy of the rules. If a printed version would be expensive to distribute, consider alternatives such as publishing the rules using the Internet, or printing one copy which is posted on the group's noticeboard. An example:

Some (fictional) solicitors decide to form a group to put on legal dramas, like Agatha Christie's *Witness for the Prosecution*. They decide to call the group the 'Amateur Drama Society for Lawyers', or 'ADSL' for short. They decide (at this time) not to form a limited company or register as a charity. The first part of its rule book might look like this:

1 The Society shall be called 'The Amateur Drama Society for Lawyers', or 'ADSL'.

2 The objects of the Society shall be:
to encourage the performance of dramatic works by amateurs
to provide or hire a theatre and all other facilities necessary for the performance of dramatic works
to provide social facilities for its members.

3 To achieve these objects, the Society, by its committee, shall have the following powers:
to promote plays and other dramatic works
to purchase or acquire interests in the copyright of dramatic works
to purchase or acquire land, buildings, plants, machinery, scenery, costumes and all other necessary effects
to raise funds, and receive subscriptions, donations and gifts
to do anything else which is beneficial to achieve the objects listed above

MEMBERS

The first members of an unincorporated society will be those people who attended the meeting during which it was agreed to set up the group, which may be recorded by those people signing a written constitution. The first members of a company limited by guarantee will be those who signed the memorandum and articles of association. The rules relating to membership are likely to be different from group to group. Consider how your group's governing document should deal with the following:

- different types of membership (members, junior members, friends, patrons etc.)
- eligibility criteria (pay annual subscription, agree to the objects of the group, age restrictions, proposed and seconded by existing members, live in a defined area, belong to a particular trade or profession)
- application process (application form, audition, whether a committee has a discretion to accept or decline membership)
- rights of membership (to attend meetings and to vote)
- ending membership (resignation, expulsion)

Different types of members may have different rights. For example, 'Friends' of a theatre group might be allowed to attend meetings but not have a right to vote. If the governing document does not set a minimum age, then any person can be a full member. In general, a group cannot seek to limit membership on the basis of race, sex or disability. The right for a society to exclude from its membership persons who the society thought would damage its objectives has been reaffirmed following a challenge under the Human Rights Act.

ADSL's rule book might say:

4 Anyone who is a qualified solicitor or works within the legal profession may apply in writing to the Society's Secretary to become a full member. Anyone who is a law student at graduate

or undergraduate level may apply in writing to the Society's Secretary to become a student member.

5 Election to membership shall be in the discretion of the Committee.

6 A full member shall pay an annual subscription fee of £10, on joining the Society and on 1 April of each year. A student member shall pay an annual subscription fee of £5 on the same dates.

7 Committee members may elect any person as an honorary life member as they may think fit and they shall be entitled to all the benefits of membership except they shall not be entitled to vote at meetings of the Society.

8 A member shall cease to be a member if he or she resigns in writing or if his or her subscription is more than 30 days in arrears, in which case that member will be deemed to have resigned.

9 The Committee may expel a member if, in their opinion, it would not be in the best interests of the Society for that person to remain a member. The Committee must follow the grievance procedure set out in its policy document as amended by the membership at a general meeting from time to time.

THE GOVERNING BODY

The members normally elect a governing body and delegate the running of the group to that committee on their behalf. Especially in smaller groups, the distinction between the governing body and members may be difficult to spot. The term 'officer' includes the role of chairperson, treasurer, secretary and any other position with special responsibilities. For companies, 'officer' means director, company secretary and perhaps shadow directors or other senior employees who run the company as if they were appointed officers. The governing document should therefore make it clear which people make up the group's governing body. It may be helpful to refer to the 'honorary' secretary if this is a different person to the company secretary. The governing document will normally state which officers should be elected and by whom. Some posts, like president, might be described as a figurehead only, with no voting or other rights.

An unincorporated association's rule book will normally state that the members must elect a governing body, who will be able to make decisions on behalf of the general membership. By definition, a group must be two or more people, but there are no general rules relating to the size of the committee. The rule book will normally set out the minimum requirements for committee membership, and the selection and appointment procedures. It may be possible for existing committee members to co-opt other members on to the governing body. The rule book should also state how the committee members leave the governing body (for example: by retirement at annual general meeting, resignation, incapacity, misconduct or non-attendance). The members normally reserve the right to remove a committee member at any time.

ADSL's rule book might say:

10 The Committee shall be the Chair, Secretary, Treasurer and other elected members. All Committee members must be elected by ballot each year at the Society's Annual General Meeting. The Committee may co-opt up to three members who shall be Committee members until the next Annual General Meeting.

For companies limited by guarantee, the members of the managing committee will be directors and will be subject to company legislation. Companies House must be notified of the details of the directors and any changes to those details. There must be at least two officers: one company director and one company secretary. If there are two or more directors, one of the directors can also be the company secretary. There is normally no maximum number of directors, but this could be altered by the group. There is no minimum age limit, but in practice no one under eighteen should be a director. Check with Companies House for other ineligible persons. The governing body, consisting of the officers, is often called the board of directors.

Charities normally need at least two trustees, and the Charity Commission (for charities in England and Wales) generally requires at least three. Trustees of registered charities must be at least eighteen years old and must not be disqualified from serving (bankruptcy, certain criminal convictions, etc.).

OTHER FORMATION ISSUES

The group will need an address for administrative purposes. Companies have to notify Companies House of a registered office and (in England and Wales) the Charity Commissioners must be informed of a contact address.

A bank will need to be given this address, together with a copy of the group's governing document (and copy of a company's certificate of incorporation), if the group requires a bank account. The bank will suggest the wording for a resolution to be passed by the governing committee to authorise the bank to take instructions from a fixed number of committee members. It is normal for every cheque to be signed by at least two committee members as a safeguard against fraud.

It will be necessary to choose a date on which the group's accounts are drawn up each year. Other policies, including equal opportunities, health and safety and data protection, should also be put into place.

Making Decisions

In the excitement of bringing together a group of people to work towards putting on a show, it is sometimes difficult to remember that the organisation must operate for the good of its whole membership and not just those who happen to be actively involved in the project in hand. There is often a delicate balance between involving everyone in the decision-making process and the need to address an issue within time constraints. The governing documents for companies limited by guarantee include by default regulations relating to the decision-making processes. However, these can be changed by the membership by following the processes set out below. Similarly, the common law has set down some basic principles relating to unincorporated associations, but any special rules set down in the governing document will normally take precedence.

MEMBERS' MEETINGS

The power to make decisions lies with all of the members. Decisions are made during members' meetings. These may be called general meetings, ordinary meetings, extraordinary meetings or special meetings. Companies limited by guarantee must hold at least one members' meeting – the annual general meeting – each year. Other types of group are not legally obliged to hold any type of members' meeting, but it would be advisable to include in the governing document the following as a minimum:

- the number of members' meetings that should take place in any year

- how to call a members' meeting
- who should receive notice of the meeting (and the effect of anyone accidentally not receiving a notice)
- who is allowed to attend and vote

ADSL's constitution might read:

11 The Annual General Meeting will be held each year in May to receive the Chair's report of the Society's activities during the last year; receive and consider the accounts and the Auditor's report; to receive the Treasurer's report; to elect an Auditor to hold office for the next year; to elect Officers and other members of the Committee and any other business proposed by the members.

12 Nominations for Committee posts must be proposed and seconded in writing and received by the Secretary seven days before the meeting. Notice of any other resolution must also be made in writing and received by the Secretary seven days before the meeting.

13 Extraordinary General Meetings may be called by the Committee at any time or within 28 days of receipt by the Secretary of a written request from at least 10% of the members stating the purpose of the required meeting and any resolutions proposed.

A meeting will not be valid unless a notice is given to everyone who is entitled to receive it. Accidental non-receipt will not affect the validity of the meeting if the governing document allows for the situation. 'Reasonable' notice must be given. If the governing document does not define 'reasonable', it will depend on the relevant circumstances. Companies limited by guarantee must give at least twenty-one clear days' notice before very important decisions are made. Other decisions can be made after fourteen clear days' notice. The notice should set out the time, date and venue for the meeting, and a summary of the matters that will be discussed. The notice should be signed and dated. Once properly convened, the meeting must be legally constituted and properly held. This means that there must be:

- someone appointed chairperson for that meeting
- the number attending the meeting (and perhaps present at decisions) must be more than the minimum number (quorum) set out in the governing document. If no minimum is set down, the default quorum will be 50% of the group's members. Sometimes members who have a conflict of interest with the interests of the group cannot count in the quorum
- any special rules set out in the governing document must be complied with, and if incorporated, the relevant rules in the Companies Act must be followed

For ADSL:

14 The Secretary shall send written notice of each General Meeting to every member at that member's last known address at least 21 days before the meeting. Accidental omission shall not invalidate any meeting.

15 The quorum for General Meetings shall be 5 or 25% of the membership, whichever is the greater.

16 The Chair, or, if absent, any other member nominated by the Committee, shall chair every General Meeting. Each member present shall have one vote. A motion will be passed if 50% or more votes are in favour of that resolution. If the votes are cast equally, the Chair shall have a casting vote.

THE POWER TO MAKE DECISIONS

Most groups delegate the day-to-day decision-making to its governing body. The procedures for holding committee meetings are similar to members' meetings, but may be subject to extra rules set out in the Companies Act (if incorporated) and/or the governing document. These special rules may set out the frequency of the meetings; how much notice should be given for meetings; who should chair the meeting; and any requirements relating to quorum.

If a person, committee or subcommittee has not been properly authorised to take decisions on behalf of everybody, then the power to make that decision remains with the general membership. Whoever has authority to make decisions in relation to a particular subject must follow the regulations set down by the group (and the Companies Act if incorporated).

If everyone agrees to a course of action, then the proposal (or motion) will be carried. Most decisions will be made in this way – if no one member objects to the proposal. If someone objects, or the members are dealing with a particularly difficult or complex point, the decision may be formally made by calling for a vote. Voting can take place by a show of hands, by members answering the question 'all those in favour?' or by written ballot. Governing documents should set out a voting procedure. Most decisions will be made if a simple majority vote of the members present and voting at the meeting are in favour of the motion. In the case of equality of voting, the governing document may set down whether the chair of the meeting has a casting vote. The governing document may set down some situations where a larger majority is required. The Companies Act requires some decisions (such as changes to the articles of association) to be passed by at least 75% of the members voting.

The chairperson has a responsibility to make sure meetings are held properly, and generally act in the best interest of the group. However, unless the governing document stipulates otherwise, the chair has no special decision-making powers, other than a possible casting vote.

Sometimes, it is not possible to follow the rules: a decision may be needed at short notice, or at times when it is not possible to consult everybody. It may be impossible to make a decision because a properly called meeting is not quorate. The rules may set out alternatives to formally called and held meetings – it may be possible to hold a meeting by telephone, or by sending a letter to everyone concerned, asking them to sign and return the proposal in order for it to take effect. If no alternatives are set down, the person or committee making the decision may ask the members to consent to the decision afterwards. This is called ratification and works on the basis that if the members consent to a technical breach of the rules, then the members cannot complain of the breach at a later date.

A proper record (or minutes) of meetings and decisions should be kept for future reference. Incorporated companies must keep minutes and some must be filed at Companies House to keep the public record up to date.

CHANGING THE CONSTITUTION

The procedure for changing the rule book should be included in the governing document. This type of decision is often reached following a special procedure, which could involve calling a special meeting after a longer notice period and requiring a higher percentage of members voting to be in favour before any change is adopted. Incorporated companies need to follow the Companies Act regulations relating to special resolutions. Charities will require consent from the Charity Commissioners in England and Wales or the Inland Revenue in Scotland before any amendment to the group's name or objects can take effect.

For ADSL:

17 The Committee may make, repeal or change any policies they may consider necessary for the benefit of the Society, which shall have effect unless set aside by the Committee or the general membership at a General Meeting.

18 These rules may be altered by resolution at any General Meeting provided that the resolution is passed by a majority of at least 75% of the members present at the meeting.

The new rules should be made available to all members (and incorporated companies must file the new articles at Companies House). The group's bankers may also insist that they are informed of any alterations.

MISCONDUCT OF MEMBERS OR OFFICERS

Members of incorporated companies can remove an officer by calling a meeting at twenty-one days' notice and voting in favour of the dismissal by simple majority. The members of an unincorporated association will only be able to make a decision to remove a member if there is a specific power to do so in the governing document. If no specific power exists, the members will need to alter the constitution first, to set down a procedure and after the procedure has been adopted, it can then be followed.

In all cases, and especially with the current focus on an individual's human rights, the person to be removed should be given the chance to put his or her view to those making the decision. If action needs to be taken before a meeting takes place, the governing body may have power to take limited action, such as altering a bank mandate for cheque signing, if that member is guilty of misusing the group's funds.

ENTERING INTO LEGALLY BINDING CONTRACTS

Some obligations will be entered into voluntarily. The group will enter into agreements (also called contracts) with many people in the course of presenting a show, not least of which will be every audience member. Most agreements do not need to be in writing to be legally enforceable – we do not write down our order at a fast-food restaurant, but we would be entitled to our money back if the restaurant did not supply the meal ordered. Note that an agreement could be made up of a combination of written terms, terms agreed verbally and terms implied by statute or courts. However, it will be easier to prove the terms of an agreement if it is recorded in permanent form. At least try to make sure that the most important parts of the agreement are in writing.

If all the terms of an agreement are clear from the outset and each party to a contract is aware of their obligations to the other party, many of the disagreements and problems that occur could be avoided. Make sure:

- a group knows who can enter into agreements on its behalf
- the person who enters into the agreement knows all of the terms that apply
- any documentation is properly drafted and does not contain blanks
- dates, times, quantities and costs are all made clear
- the effect of termination is known
- records are kept of all of the terms of the group's legally binding obligations

Members delegate the day-to-day running of an organisation to its management committee. In turn, the committee may need to delegate some decision-making. A treasurer or ticket secretary would find it hard to operate if they had to obtain the committee's approval for every single ticket sale before the transaction was completed. Conversely, many members of the committee would be quite rightly upset to learn that one committee member had made a commitment on behalf of the group (for example, the purchase of expensive equipment) without prior consultation. A stranger can normally rely on a statement from a committee member that s/he has the authority of the committee to enter into a legally binding agreement on behalf of the group. Policies and procedures must therefore be set down, so that all committee members know how much authority they have at any one time in relation to any area of responsibility. If a committee member exceeds their authority, it may be possible to ensure that that committee member becomes personally responsible for any liabilities that flow from their actions.

To be legally binding, an agreement must be between at least two parties who intend to create an enforceable arrangement. A purely domestic arrangement (such as a promise to meet a friend for an after-show party) is not legally binding. Each agreement will consist of an offer, the acceptance of that offer and some form of consideration passing between the parties. A wish or intention (for example, a general enquiry as to whether a venue is available for booking) will not be an offer. Adverts are not normally offers unless they are very specific. Once made, an offer can be accepted until it is withdrawn (for example, a promise to reserve tickets for a show for seven days lapses on the eighth day). Negotiation can take place, and once all parties are happy with all of the terms, the offer will be accepted. If some form of consideration has passed between the parties, the contract will then be binding. Consideration is usually a cash payment (for example, the price of a ticket), but it need not be so. A landlord might be willing to hire a scenery store to the group for free if the group paints and repairs it. Something of value is present, and the contract is therefore binding. The consideration need not be full market value to be valid – a local authority might allow a group to hire a venue for a nominal sum, well below the market price. In summary, a contract does not need to be 'a good deal' – a group will receive no protection from the courts if it has entered into a financially bad agreement of its own volition. Some terms, especially relating to the exclusion or restriction of liability, are subject to a fairness test. See below for more details.

Some contracts, including land sales and the buying and selling of copyrights have to be in writing. A summary of the terms of employment contracts should also be made available in writing. However, most arrangements do not need to be in writing or signed to be legally binding. An exchange of letters, or a telephone call (or a combination of both) may be enough to create a contract.

Up until May 2000, it was difficult for anyone who was not a party to a contract to enforce any of its terms. It is now possible, under the Contracts (Rights of Third Parties) Act, 1999, for a third party who benefits from a contract to take legal action to enforce its terms. It is possible to narrow the scope of contracts to restrict this right, and therefore careful consideration should be given to any contracts that involve third parties. If in any doubt, and especially if the agreement is of high value, seek legal advice.

EXCLUDING OR LIMITING LIABILITY

Most contracts that your group is asked to sign will include a set of standard terms and conditions. It is likely that those terms will include a paragraph which tries to exclude or limit the liability to the group if the agreement goes wrong and the group suffers a loss. However, any statement which attempts to exclude liability for death or personal injury arising from the contractor's negligence will not be effective. Other limitations may only be binding if they pass a fairness or reasonableness test, depending on whether it is a consumer or business transaction. Similarly, any statement that your group wishes to make to limit liability must be carefully written if it is to be effective. Consider taking legal advice before relying on a limitation clause.

LATE PAYMENTS

Since 1998, under the Late Payment of Commercial Debts (Interest) Act, all businesses and voluntary organisations have a statutory right to charge interest on debts if they employ fifty or fewer employees. Interest can be charged from the date the payment should have been made, or, if no date was agreed, thirty days after the invoice date or the delivery of the goods or services (whichever is the later). The current rate of interest (unless any other rate is agreed) is 8% above the base rate.

LEGAL PROCEEDINGS

It is a fact of life that sometimes even the best laid plans go wrong. In these cases, a group may wish to terminate a contract to avoid large liabilities. First, check the terms of the contract, since the ability to terminate early may be an express term. If not, it may be possible to walk away from the contract if the other party has fundamentally breached the terms – i.e. a breach that is so serious that the whole contract fails. If not, a contract can always be altered with the agreement of all parties.

In rare cases, it may not be possible for a disagreement to be settled amicably. The group's internal procedures may have broken down, or it may be unable to resolve an issue with a supplier of goods or services. The group may therefore need to commence legal proceedings (for example, to recover its property being held unlawfully by a member or outsider) or it may be subject to legal proceedings (for example, a landlord may sue to recover rent that the group has not paid). Either way, the party in the wrong may be ordered to pay damages, which aim to put the innocent party into the same position that it would have been in if the arrangement had been honoured.

Remember that claims can arise in situations other than contract disputes. A breach of a duty of care, or claim of negligence or other statutory default could all lead to an order to pay damages, and perhaps some other form of relief, including a promise not to carry out a particular action. Even more importantly, some breaches lead to criminal liability.

Taking a case to court is expensive – in terms of cash, time and morale. Careful consideration must be given to the circumstances, after taking legal advice. Alternatives may be mediation or arbitration in accordance with the Arbitration Act 1996.

FOLLOWING BEST PRACTICE

The concept of best practice is no more than an acknowledgement that there may be more than one way of reaching a decision or working on a project, and that the group should aim to use the highest quality way of achieving that goal. This is in stark contrast to the 'cheap and cheerful' school of thought, which can so easily discount other non-financial factors in the decision-making processes. It recognises that there will be situations where cost or time constraints will impact on decisions made, but nevertheless choices should be made taking into account all the relevant factors.

For each important decision, the group should aim to complete some initial information gathering to make sure the decision can be taken after considering all relevant factors. The decision-making process should be clear and concise. The decision should be recorded, acted upon and, possibly, reviewed to make sure everything went to plan. The following sections highlight some sources of help and advice, and ways of minimising the risk of unforeseen liabilities. Remember that members of the group may have lots of experience to draw on, but even with this valuable resource, there may be times when advice from an independent body could be worth considering.

Seeking Advice

It is likely that someone in another local group may have experiences similar to your own and may be able to provide some help or assistance.

AFFILIATIONS

Look for umbrella organisations which bring together groups with similar aims and objectives. Also look for groups from different backgrounds, but with a common thread – your group may gain from attending meetings arranged locally for all voluntary organisations, where the only common theme is that all member groups are based in the same region. This type of meeting may give you access to funding opportunities that even a specialist international organisation may not have knowledge of.

One of the largest and oldest umbrella organisations devoted to the amateur stage is the National Operatic and Dramatic Association (NODA), which was founded in 1899 'to protect and advance the interests of Operatic and Dramatic Art, and of Societies engaged therein'. It has a membership of some 2,300 amateur societies and 2,500 individual enthusiasts throughout the UK, staging musicals, operas, plays, concerts and pantomimes in a wide variety of performing venues, ranging from the country's leading professional theatres to tiny village halls.

NODA is divided into eleven areas, each headed by an area councillor who sits on the National Council (the ruling body of the association), supported by a network of regional representatives. The association is administered from its headquarters in London, with a knowledgeable and friendly staff able to deal with enquiries relating to amateur theatre.

NODA aims:

- to give a shared voice to the amateur sector
- to help amateur societies and individuals achieve the highest standards of best practice and performance
- to provide leadership and advice to enable the amateur sector to tackle the challenges and opportunities of the twenty-first century

By bringing together so many smaller organisations, associations like NODA can benefit from economies of scale. NODA has access to resources that local groups cannot afford. NODA is also one of the providers of summer schools and courses, which gives members a chance to socialise as well as learn.

A selection of the larger umbrella organisations relevant to amateur theatre appear in the Reference Section at the end of this handbook. More are listed in the publications referred to in the Further Reading section.

INTERNET RESOURCES

Other alternatives for networking can be carried out from the comfort of a cyber café. A number of Internet sites have developed over the last few years. Some have dwindled and died, others have gone from strength to strength. One of the first, www.amdram.co.uk, still remains a vibrant site, constantly updated by its hard-working editor. One of the benefits of the Internet is the ability to link pieces of information. Check with some of the leading web directories to see if more specialist information you may wish to access is also available. Remember that most of the World Wide Web is unregulated, and there is no guarantee that information available on the net is accurate or up to date. Let the surfer beware!

LAWYERS AND ACCOUNTANTS

Unless a group has only a limited number of transactions in any year, or skilled professionals on its management board, it is unlikely that the members will have sufficient up-to-date knowledge and spare time to deal on a voluntary basis with all of the legal or accounting matters that are raised. All groups are likely to have a treasurer and larger groups are likely to engage a bookkeeper to maintain their accounting records, but any reasonably large group is likely to benefit from the assistance of a professionally qualified accountant. Similarly, asking for legal advice on a specialist subject may reduce costs in the long run. The most important thing is to realise that a good working relationship is based on a team approach between the group and the relevant professional. In much the same way that a committee will work better together if they feel comfortable together, a group must be confident in its professional advisers.

Legal and accountancy advice can be expensive and these professionals will normally charge an hourly rate for their services. It is therefore worthwhile following the guidelines below to minimise professional costs and to obtain maximum value for money from accountancy fees.

- Involve a professional sooner rather than later to ensure that the group's affairs are set up from the start in the most tax-efficient manner.
- Check your chosen professional has the right level of skill and experience.
- Prepare for any meetings by gathering any relevant paperwork, and agree a division of labour between the group (and its committee members) and the professional.
- Ask for an estimate and, if possible, agree a fixed fee for the agreed work to be undertaken and monitor costs carefully to avoid unexpected bills. Although the cost of professional fees will always be a factor, remember that the cheapest is not necessarily the best.

Arrange for records to be maintained by the group. A solicitor may need to see paperwork before any advice can be given. Keeping accounting records is likely to be cheaper than using an accountant's staff to do the work. There are many computer accounts packages available – your accountant should advise on which one to use. This will enable the generation of quarterly VAT returns and draft annual accounts which will form part of the group's tax return.

Keeping Records

Failing to keep comprehensive records may save time in the short run, but will create problems in the future. The officers are in a position of trust and responsibility, and they should be able to demonstrate, at any time, that they have discharged their role with care and attention. Written records reduce the possible areas for uncertainty and therefore reduce the risk of everything from time-wasting to fraud. Regardless of the statutory duties that a group or its officers may be under, it is suggested that all groups should aim to keep accurate membership records, accounts and minutes of meetings. Not only will these records help in the smooth running of the group, but they may be required by outside funders or government bodies. Beware of destroying records – a group may be liable for something that took place twelve years ago.

As the effects of Lottery-funded projects are felt, it is likely that more organisations will be obliged to prepare detailed accounts and financial reports to justify funding applications. Other external bodies, such as sponsors, may also require statistics to prove the success of a particular scheme.

KEEPING ACCOUNTS

All groups should keep accounts, and for all charities and companies there is a legal requirement to do so. Charities with annual income and expenditure of more than £10,000 must prepare audited accounts, which must be submitted to the Charity Commission (or the Charities division of the Inland Revenue for Scottish charities). A new Statement of Recommended Practice (SORP) for drawing up accounts was issued in October 2000, which is mandatory for accounting periods commencing after 1 January 2001.

Limited companies must always file accounts with Companies House, and may have to prepare audited accounts depending on the company's governing document, but subject always to audit if the company is of a defined size (over £90,000 for charitable companies, or £1 million turnover, or £1.4 million assets for non-charity companies – 2000/2001). Charities must keep their records for at least six years, and this is advisable for other types of organisation.

For unincorporated associations, the governing document may make it clear that the primary responsibility for keeping the accounts lies with the treasurer. The rules may also set out on which date the accounts should run from each year (typically from 1 April to match the financial year but another date may be more appropriate depending on show dates). The rules will also normally state who may operate the group's bank account and sign cheques. Some organisations will be under a duty for their accounts to be formally checked by an auditor, and some others volunteer their books for audit as a means of double-checking.

THE CONSTITUTION

Companies must have a written constitution, open to inspection by anyone. Unincorporated associations do not necessarily need a written constitution, but, for the reasons given above, should aim to do so. Once in a written form, it is important that the constitution is kept up to date, with any agreed amendments being included.

SPECIAL RULES FOR LIMITED COMPANIES AND CHARITIES

The name shown on the Certificate of Incorporation must be used on all company documents, together with its registration number and registered office. It is not necessary to list the directors on company documents, but it is not permissible to list only a proportion of the names – it must be all or none. So, an honorary president's name can only appear in isolation if s/he is not a director. A company must keep some of its records publicly available. These include the register of members, directors, company secretaries, minutes of members' meetings and accounting records. It is advisable to check the statutory requirements for record keeping on incorporation, and regularly afterwards, since if the regulations are not met, the officers may be personally fined.

A charitable organisation normally has to include an indication of its charitable status if its name does not include 'charity' or 'charitable'. They are also given a registration number which should be quoted. A charity is also under a statutory duty to keep accurate financial records, as well as records relating to its structure for at least six years.

VAT REGISTRATION

All organisations registered for VAT must include their name, address and VAT registration number on invoices and receipts. All VAT receipts for expenditure must be kept; returns completed and records retained for at least six years.

CONFIDENTIALITY AND THE DATA PROTECTION ACT

It may seem strange to look at the concept of confidentiality in relation to a group that performs in public. However, it is likely that some of the group's activities would be regarded by its members as private, such as secret ballots for elections of the office holders, or their ex-directory telephone numbers. It should be made clear that there will be some situations that the group will be under an overriding duty to disclose. These may include:

- following a breach of a duty of care (especially in relation to children)
- when the group is subject to a statutory duty to disclose (to report drug trafficking or money laundering, etc.)
- when the group has agreed to a contractual promise to disclose (a copyright licence agreement may require box-office figures)

Some of the group's records (if incorporated or charitable) will be open to inspection by the public. In other cases, the group may decide to make some of its information public. If it does, it should be sure that no duty of confidentiality is breached. Some contracts include confidentiality clauses, and if the contractual duty of confidentiality is breached, the group may be liable for damages. In other situations, information may have been passed to the group with a clear intention that the information should remain secret.

We perform each year at the local theatre, during the week before the professional Christmas show starts. We make the booking in June of each year and the theatre manager often tells our secretary which show the professionals will perform to make sure we do not clash. Because the press releases have not been prepared, the theatre manager asks us to keep the information secret until the season's programme has been made public.

The Data Protection Act, 1988, is a complicated statute. A six-year transitional period ends on 23 October 2007, but most of the activities covered by the Act will be in force from October 2001. Voluntary groups have nothing to fear from this legislation. Its aim is to give people ('Data Subjects') some form of control over how their personal information is used and stored. If the group uses personal data (whether by computer or by paper files) it must collect, record, use, retrieve, disclose, adapt, alter, combine and destroy it in a fair and responsible way. Personal data can only be used if the individual has consented to its use, knows who is using the information and whether the data will be passed on to anyone else. Examples of personal data include membership records and mailing lists.

All groups will be automatically under a duty to comply with this legislation. However, some groups will not need to notify the Office of the Information Commissioner (who used to be called the Data Protection Commissioner) that they use personal data. If a group holds only manual data (i.e. not computerised) or it only holds computerised membership records, it may be excused from the notification process if the members have consented to the group holding records and the records are used only to send information to the members. It is important that the group checks these exemptions carefully, because failure to notify could lead to a criminal offence. Voluntary notification should be considered. It is worth repeating that a group will be subject to the provisions of the Act regardless of whether the group has to notify the Information Commissioner. This is different to the old regulations contained in the Data Protection Act, 1984, which only related to computer records.

Data can only be processed if at least one of a limited number of conditions is fulfilled:

- the person who is the subject of the information (the Data Subject) has given their consent
- the data processing is necessary to perform a contract with that Data Subject or some other legal obligation
- the data processing is necessary to protect the Data Subject or carry out public functions
- the data processing is required to meet the legitimate interests of the processor or other defined third parties

All Data Subjects must be told that their data is being collected and how it will be used. Specific reference must be made if the data will be used by anyone else. This means that any questionnaires or ticket-booking forms should clearly state how the information is going to be stored, used and disseminated. Any form should include a box which allows the Data Subject to opt in to further mailings. If your group is going to share a mailing list with another group, this should be made clear to the Data Subjects. Alternatively, you could offer to include information from another group in your group's mailing. This second method does not involve handing any data to another group and may be less objectionable to those people who do not wish to have their details given to third parties.

If your group's records have been created since October 1998, they must comply with these rules immediately. If they were held on a computerised system before that date, they must comply from October 2001. Manual systems used before that date do not have to comply until October 2007. Consider sending a letter to all members asking if they wish to continue to be on your group's mailing list, or if they object to your group sharing their details with other groups (if relevant).

Regardless of when the records have to comply, Data Subjects have the right to see information concerning them held by the group. Therefore make sure that all records, including audition comments, would not cause embarrassment.

Special rules apply to 'sensitive data'. This includes information relating to racial or ethnic origin, political opinions, religious beliefs, health, sex life and criminal proceedings and convictions. The Data Subject must give explicit consent to the use of sensitive data, unless it is being collected for the sole purpose of ethnic monitoring for equal opportunity policies. Alternatives should be explored, including separating sensitive data so that it can be submitted and processed anonymously.

All data should be kept in a safe place, and should also be kept up to date. It should not be stored for longer than necessary, so that any sensitive data should be destroyed after any equal opportunities monitoring has taken place. Some umbrella organisations produce model rules which contain minimum standards for data protection. If not, the Information Commissioner can provide detailed guidance.

Liability of Members and Officers

Some of the group's obligations are not voluntary – the group must comply with common law rules and statutory obligations. The group must take into account the risk of being found liable for its actions (or defaults) in this wider sense. It is not correct to believe that by making no decisions at all, the group can avoid all liabilities.

It is worth stating at this point that the vast majority of groups never reach a position when a member or officer faces a situation when s/he has to pay a debt on behalf of the group, or is held responsible for an offence committed by the group. A group will normally plan for liabilities and will have sufficient funds to pay for those liabilities – for example, a group may enter into an arrangement to hire a venue for £500, payable one week before the performance date. No member or officer will be concerned about this transaction if the group has £500 in its reserves on the payment date.

There are a small number of particular circumstances where officers and members may become responsible for an action taken (or not taken) by the group, its governing body, its officers, members or employees. These include:

CRIMINAL OFFENCES OR BREACHES OF STATUTORY DUTY

Failure to comply with health and safety legislation, entertainment licensing requirements or failure to comply with the Companies Acts or Charities Act, or, in Scotland, the Law Reform (Miscellaneous Provisions) (Scotland) Act, 1990, are all examples of this type of breach. The person or company that commits the criminal act or breach of duty is primarily liable. Officers may be liable for their own and each other's actions. Members may be liable if they took part, or authorised the action or breach by instructing someone to commit the offence or breach.

BREACH OF TRUST

This may occur if an officer steals from the group, makes an un-authorised profit from the group, causes a loss through mis-management or allows the group's funds to be used for a purpose which was not authorised. The officer will be primarily liable.

BREACH OF CONTRACT

This may occur if the group cannot pay for goods or services received, it cannot provide a service it has promised (e.g. a show to its audience) or it has breached other terms of an agreement (e.g. returning hired goods in a damaged state). For incorporated associations, it is the company that enters into the contract. As long as the group has power to enter into the contract, and the person who makes the arrangements on behalf of the group had authority to do so, then no liability will rest with the individuals. For unincorporated associations, it will be individual members entering into contracts on behalf of the group. Those individuals will be primarily responsible, but they might be able to reclaim any loss from other officers or other members depending on who authorised the agreement.

NEGLIGENCE, PASSING OFF OR OTHER TORTIOUS ACTS

A 'tort', or 'delict' in Scotland (a legal word for 'wrong'), can lead to liability if the action causes injury, loss or damage. Some torts can also be criminal offences. Negligence, defamation, nuisance and passing off are all examples of torts. An injury to an actor caused by lack of proper supervision may lead to a claim for negligence. Using the name of another company to try to lure audience members to a show could lead to a claim for passing off. Normally the person committing the tort will be primarily liable. Others authorising it may also share responsibility.

SUMMARY

Who is ultimately liable may depend upon whether the group is an incorporated or unincorporated association, and whether anyone authorised the action (or inaction) which created the liability. Liability can be passed to third parties in unexpected ways (an employer may automatically be responsible for the acts of an employee) and liability can be shared between a group of people. The best way of limiting liability is to make sure the group's responsibilities are clear, to fulfil those obligations on time and to keep records to prove compliance.

Insurance

From the first audition to the end-of-show party and all the fund-raising events in between, the participants, volunteers and even the audience are constantly at risk. Checking that the group undertakes these activities using 'best practice' will minimise the risk but there is still a possibility that significant loss or injury might occur.

Correctly insuring your production is vitally important. Some types of insurance are mandatory, others are voluntary. When looking for insurance to cover your next production, consider a package that has been specifically designed with amateur theatre groups in mind. These will include wide-ranging protection and will often have specially written policies to deal with areas that concern theatre groups primarily. The alternative will be to enter into separate arrangements with different underwriters and hope to have everything covered. This is likely to be a more expensive route.

Insurance policies are contracts of the utmost good faith. Any factor which may be relevant to the insurer must be disclosed. If it is not, the policy may be cancelled by the insurer.

Key areas for insurance are:

- **Public liability**: This covers liability for illness, injury or death of members of the public (excluding those your group has employed) and for damage to their property caused by the group's negligence. In the litigious day and age that we live in, make sure that you have a minimum level of cover of £2 million and that the policy can be increased if required. Some local authorities may insist on £5 million, and in extreme cases, £10 million, as a precondition to granting an entertainment licence. Also check whether all group members, including members of the governing body, are covered by this insurance. Consider drawing any specific limitations to the members' attention.

- **Employers' liability**: This covers liability for incidents causing illness, injury or death to employees. Every employer must have this type of insurance. Remember that the definition of 'employee' under the relevant legislation is wide and contractors or self-employed people used by the group may trigger the need for this type of insurance. If in doubt whether a volunteer could be found to be an employee, take specialist advice.

- **Personal accident insurance**: This covers accidents not due to the group's negligence which cause illness, injury or death. Check if special cover is required for unusual fund-raising events like sponsored swims, etc. If members of a charitable governing body are included for this type of cover, permission must be sought from the Charity Commission.

- **Property**: This will include damage caused to land and buildings, but may also cover sets, props, equipment and other valuable items used in a show and perhaps while in transit. If the group owns or leases buildings, check that the group has cover for injury caused to anyone using the building. Cover may also be possible for assets (such as computers) which are used by committee members.

- **Money**: This will help recover the loss or theft of money while in the hands or occupied dwellings of the group's officials.

- **Vehicles**: A group that owns vehicles or uses vehicles owned by third parties must ensure that they are properly insured. No vehicle can be used on public roads unless it is insured for injury or death to passengers, third parties and third-party property.

- **Abandonment**: This basically covers the loss of expense due to the show being unable to go ahead. Check for outdoor events to see if cancellation due to weather conditions is covered.

- **Fidelity guarantee**: This covers against loss resulting from an act of fraud or dishonesty by key members of your society. Cover may include accidental breach of copyright and loss of documents.

And don't forget, it's not only the performing members of the society that need insurance cover. Those helping backstage and front-of-house, people employed to erect the scenery and wire up the lighting should be covered. All of these volunteers should be encouraged to become members of the group so that they will be able to benefit from any insurance which applies to members only.

Contractors should have their own public liability insurance and professional liability insurance. A group may wish to check – especially if the contractor is involved in high-risk activities such as 'flying' or other special effects.

It will only be possible to enter into a contract of insurance if the group has power to do so. Unless the group's governing document specifically includes a power to insure, it may be necessary to rely on general powers granted by statute to companies and charities. If in doubt, take specialist advice, because any action taken without sufficient power may be void and unenforceable. Once taken out, a policy should be regularly reviewed. Always check the specific exclusions, which may include an upper and lower age limit. Also remember that no cover will be available if the premiums are not kept up to date or if the insurers are not notified of any changes.

Remember to keep the insurance policy in a safe place, and do not destroy it at the end of its term. A person who suffers an injury or loss has several years to bring a claim against the group. Also consider keeping an inventory of all of the assets owned by the group, perhaps with photographs, in case your group has to make a claim. An inventory will help negotiations with the insurance company's loss adjuster.

Fund-raising

INTRODUCTION

The best fund-raising schemes are fun to organise and some offer something to the donors in return for their contribution. That return might be the chance to win a prize, or the opportunity to be associated with a successful group which has a good profile among its loyal fan base and in the wider community. This section summarises some of the most popular fund-raising events, but some of the most successful activities in the past have also been the most innovative.

There is a general principle that funds raised for one purpose must not be used for any other purpose. It may therefore be necessary to identify in a group's financial records particular restricted cash reserves for special purposes. If a group is going to undertake a special fund-raising appeal for a particular purpose, decide what will happen to the funds raised if the required amount is not raised.

> My group started to raise funds for a new roof for its theatre, but by the time we raised the required target, the cost of the new roof had increased. This happened several times, and we have now decided it will be uneconomical to continue to perform in the building. However, because we made it clear to all donors that the funds raised would be used to purchase a new building if the roof appeal failed, we have been able to use the collected funds to kick-start a new fund-raising appeal.

If a group cannot fulfil the particular purpose quoted to donors, and does not make it clear to donors that the funds may be used for other purposes, then the group is legally obliged to return the funds (or surplus funds if too much has been raised) to the donors. If this is not possible, and the group is a registered charity, the Charity Commissioners can supervise a special scheme for the proceeds.

SPONSORSHIP

There are two types of sponsorship: sponsorship for money and sponsorship in kind (where a company provides equipment, props, costumes or other goods for free). The sponsor may just want to be associated with a production, but always find out if the sponsor wants anything else in return. Companies often take months to make decisions about spending money in this way, so start looking for sponsors as soon as possible. If the business does not want anything in return, this will be a donation and treated differently for tax purposes.

Ask around the group to see if anyone has any contacts in local companies. If a member can introduce the group to the business, the chances of success are probably higher. Retired members of the group may also be members of the local Chamber of Commerce or Rotary club and know people who run local companies. Consider planning a sponsorship campaign around your particular show. Are there any themes that might appeal to a certain local company? On the other hand, your group's show may contain material which might offend or be too controversial. You do not want a butcher who has agreed to support your group to be offended because the play is advocating vegetarianism!

Remember the sponsor will gain from a sponsorship package. For example, tickets for the opening night, a logo on leaflets and posters, and a page in your programme will all be worth something to your sponsor. If your group has a mailing list, you can mention the sponsor next time a newsletter is sent out. This may be an easier way of bringing the sponsor to the notice of the members than allowing the sponsor access to the group's database, which may infringe the Data Protection Act rules.

LOYALTY SCHEMES

The simplest loyalty scheme is charging a membership fee. Your governing document may allow you to levy a yearly subscription. In addition, if you are an established group and you are building up a marketing list, you may want to introduce a loyalty scheme to help raise funds. This could take the form of a newsletter or a priority booking mailing list. You could offer these 'friends' of the group a chance to meet the cast after the show or reduced ticket prices or a free drink when they get to the venue. If the group has a loyal and enthusiastic following, they may be willing to pay for these perks. You may also be able to seek volunteers to run a coffee bar before the show and during the interval, with all the proceeds going to the group. If you serve any food or drink, make sure that you comply with all health and safety rules. Make the most of loyal followers, but in return make sure the group can deliver what has been promised. You don't want these people pulling out. Even if they do not ask for their money back, unhappy loyal supporters will be hard to win back.

RAISING MONEY ON THE NIGHT

Once you have a captive audience in the venue, there are still opportunities to raise money. For example, a raffle to win a prize or a prop from the show should raise more than its cost. However, lotteries are heavily regulated. The current rules are contained in the Lotteries and Amusements Act, 1976, and the Lotteries Regulations, 1977 (amended in 1993). In summary, a lottery is a game of chance, which offers prizes in return for a payment to participate.

If your group is a registered charity with an annual income over £10,000, all tickets and publicity must state its registered status. Alcohol prizes may be banned by your local licensing authority, unless special permission is granted. National lotteries, small lotteries, private lotteries and society lotteries are permitted, but any other form of lottery is illegal.

SMALL LOTTERIES

Small lotteries must take place as part of another event, such as a bazaar, sale of work, fête, dinner, dance, performance or entertainment of a similar character. The lottery cannot be the main reason why people attend the event. The regulations for this type of lottery include:

- no registration requirements
- the maximum cost of buying the prizes must be £250
- no money prizes
- no limit on number or price of tickets, but all tickets must be sold at the event
- the winners must be announced during the event
- proceeds of the event and the lottery (after costs) must not be used for private gain

PRIVATE LOTTERIES

This type of lottery is run by a group for its members. Non-members cannot take part. The group cannot be set up solely for gaming and must be authorised to run lotteries in its governing document. Regulations include:

- no registration requirements
- money prizes are allowed
- no limit on number of tickets, but tickets cannot be sold for less than their full price (so no 'buy two tickets, get one free' offers)
- no tickets can be sold by post
- tickets should show the price, the name and address of the person organising the lottery (the promoter), and a statement of the ticket restrictions (only to be sold to members/prizes only awarded to the person who purchased the winning ticket)
- no refunds

- no notices or adverts for the lottery except on the group's own premises
- proceeds of the lottery (after costs) must be used for prizes or the group's funds

SOCIETY LOTTERIES

This type of lottery takes place on behalf of a group for charitable purposes, for participation in or support of sports or games or cultural activities or other purposes as long as it is not for private gain or commercial profit. Also:

- tickets cannot be sold before the lottery is registered with the local authority or the gaming board. Register with the local authority if total ticket sales will be less than £20,000 and the total from all lotteries run by the group in any year is less than £250,000
- tickets must cost £1 or less, and all sold at the same price
- tickets must be printed with information specified in the Lotteries Regulations, including the price. Reputable printers will be aware of these rules
- no refunds
- no sales to anyone under sixteen
- special rules exist for street and door-to-door sales
- no more than 50% of proceeds can be used for prizes. No prize may be worth over £25,000 or 10% of total proceeds
- limits exist on the amount allowed for expenses
- all proceeds after costs must be used for the group's purposes
- the group will need to make a return to the licensing authority and keep proper records

FREE PRIZE DRAWS

If a group decides to hold a free prize draw, this will not be a lottery, since no payment is made to participate. However, it should be made clear that to take part, no donation is necessary. If the group 'suggests' a minimum donation, this will fulfil the payment rule and the promotion will be classed as a lottery.

COMPETITIONS

Where lotteries are games of chance, competitions involve a level of skill. That level must not be so low that everyone would be able to reach the winning stage. If more than one person could fulfil all of the requirements of the competition, it may be necessary for some form of tie-breaker. Predictions of future events (such as 'guess the number of tickets sold for the run of a show') may not be a competition, but rather a bet, which is subject to the complicated gaming rules and regulations.

An audience may enjoy a competition in the show's programme. Pose a question and ask people to post their answers to the group after the show is over. This is also a good way of building up a marketing list, as long as you make sure you are following the Data Protection regulations. The rules for the competition must be clear. The British Codes of Advertising and Sales Promotion recommends that the stated rules include:

- entry requirements (such as age restrictions, maximum number of entries per person)
- closing date
- any requirements for proof of purchase
- method of choosing a winner
- the prizes, and whether any cash alternative is available
- how and when the winners and results will be announced
- who will own the copyright in entries, and whether they will be returned
- if winners will be required to take part in any publicity

Special care should be taken if the competition is aimed at children.

GAMING

Games of chance (other than lotteries) are also subject to strict rules. Licences are always required for amusement machines. Bingo evenings, with prizes under £300 and proceeds to the group, do not need licences if the total amount paid by participants is under £3. Bingo games which take place during a bazaar, sale of work, fête, dinner, dance, etc. (as per small lotteries) do not require licences and are not subject to the restrictions above. Gaming law is complex and any group should take advice on the effects of the Gaming Act, 1968 (amended in Scotland by the Licensing (Scotland) Act, 1976). In 2000, the government announced a review of gaming and lottery law, which is yet to be published (2001).

GIFTS AND LEGACIES

As mentioned above, some people or businesses may be willing to make gifts to the group with no strings attached. Making cash donations might be tax efficient, and the group may be able to claim extra funds from the Inland Revenue for each gift received under the Gift Aid Scheme. Your group may also ask its members and friends to include the group as a beneficiary in their will. This is obviously a sensitive subject and should be handled with tact.

COLLECTIONS

A simple collection can be a low-cost way of raising funds and increasing awareness of the group's activities. Obtain the owner's permission to collect money from the inhabitants of private premises. Strict rules apply to collections from private premises if the public have a right of access, for example railway stations and shopping centres. Other street collections or door-to-door collections are also regulated. The rules vary regionally, so check with your local authority, but expect to apply at least one month in advance. The licence (if granted) will be subject to conditions including the requirement to provide the licensing authority with a statement of accounts. One group went from pub to pub to try to drum up some ticket sales for their next production, inviting people to make a donation if they were unwilling to buy a ticket. This is a house-to-house collection, which requires a licence.

The Charities Act, 1992 allows the government to introduce new rules relating to public collections, but these new regulations are not yet in force (2001).

OTHER EVENTS

Your group may organise several shows a year, but it is likely that not all of the members are involved in all of the shows. Holding fund-raising events between shows is a good way of keeping your members interested in the group's activities. A coffee morning, jumble sale or car-boot sale may not raise much money, but it may boost the morale of the organisers and supporters. If the car-boot sale is to take place on public property, the local authority must grant a licence for a 'market', unless all proceeds are for charity. If it is to take place on private land, obtain the consent of the landowner. If car-boot sales take place regularly, planning permission might be needed. It is an offence to sell goods which do not comply with the relevant consumer safety requirements. Consider banning second-hand electrical and gas appliances, and check for dangerous toys. Other items (including clothes and household goods) may have to meet safety standards.

The more daring might like to follow a trend started by the Women's Institute and print calendars featuring pictures of naked volunteers – making sure that the end result is not obscene! Selling goods could be viewed as 'trading', which may have tax ramifications. See pages 256-8 for more details.

Sponsored events are popular and can generate good publicity. They require some management to ensure that sponsorship pledges are recorded, collected and handed in. All sponsor forms should show details of the group and (outside Scotland) all charities should be named with their registered charity number. It may be necessary to reveal any expenses that are going to be incurred and deducted from the sponsorship funds – especially relevant to fund-raising expeditions or parachute jumps, where the costs can be high. Also check with the group's insurers to make sure that the event is covered.

Trips to see other shows may be popular – especially if tickets can be purchased at a group rate. It may be worth joining forces with other local groups to make these activities even more worthwhile.

GRANTS

Larger-scale fund-raising often involves applications to grant-making bodies. The Arts Councils are responsible for developing, sustaining and promoting the arts through the distribution of public money from central government and revenue generated by the National Lottery. Various funding schemes for capital and revenue projects, with different entry criteria, are available at any one time. Other charitable trusts and foundations exist with particular interests. Keeping up to date with all these schemes is a full-time occupation. Databases exist to help narrow the search for available grants, which are normally available at local libraries or umbrella organisations, including the Voluntary Arts Network.

Grants may be given for a specific purpose and may be subject to a number of conditions (matched funding, for example). Do not be surprised if your group has to report regularly in an agreed format to the grant-making body, and include this administration in the calculation of whether the application is worth making. The grant-making body may require an agreed level of recognition for its grant and may require the repayment of all or some of the grant if time spans are exceeded or other conditions not met.

LOANS

Banks and other financial institutions will normally judge a request for a loan on commercial terms. If your group is new, has erratic income, or cannot offer security to ensure repayment, the lender is unlikely to look favourably on a request for a loan. Members may be willing to lend a group some money, perhaps on the understanding that the sum will only be repaid after the ticket-sale money has been collected. These types of arrangement should be in writing to ensure that the repayment terms are understood by all parties.

CREDITING DONORS

Effective fund-raising needs to be well planned, imaginative and people-centred. Make sure those taking part feel valued, obtaining a sense of achievement from what they do. Remember to say thank you. A donor who is thanked appropriately will feel more inclined to support the group again in the future. Some groups that own their own venue place a list of donors on a noticeboard, or offer to place a plaque on one of the auditorium's seats. A simple mention in the group's annual report or newsletter may be appropriate. However, some donors prefer to remain anonymous, so get permission before any public announcement is made.

SALE OF FOOD AND DRINK

Selling refreshments may amount to trading and will in any event be subject to the Food Safety Act 1990 and the Food Safety (General Food Hygiene) Regulations 1995. The local authority's environmental health department can provide advice.

Tax

Amateur theatre groups may need to understand and deal with a range of taxes including value added tax (VAT), corporation tax, pay as you earn (PAYE), business rates and stamp duty. Tax compliance is likely to be low on the list of priorities of a group because members of the group may be unaware of the impact of these taxes. The penalties attached to getting things wrong or delivering late returns or not paying enough tax on time have become more stringent in recent years and the tax authorities will not make any allowance for the fact that they are dealing with an amateur group. Taxation is a complex area in which mistakes can be very expensive.

Unincorporated associations are treated like companies for most tax purposes. In the first instance, the group will be liable to pay the relevant tax, but if it fails to do so, the treasurer or other officer responsible for the unincorporated group's financial affairs may become personally responsible for payment. In all cases, the governing body will have final responsibility for all financial matters.

VAT

VAT was originally intended to be a 'simple tax' when it was introduced in 1973, but has since become extremely complicated. The standard rate of VAT is currently 17.5% (2001), although some goods are zero-rated and others are subject to a 5% rate. VAT is chargeable on 'supplies' made by a 'taxable person' in the course of 'business'. So a registered trader charges VAT on the goods or services sold, hired or given away ('output tax'). The trader recovers

VAT on expenditure ('input tax'). Usually, at the end of each three-month VAT return period, the trader accounts for the excess of output tax over input tax to HM Customs & Excise or receives a refund if input tax exceeds output tax.

Relevant transactions ('supplies') fall into one of four categories: standard-rated, zero-rated, exempt and outside the scope of VAT. A fifth category, relating to the reduced rate of 5%, only applies to goods and services which are outside the scope of amateur theatre companies, such as domestic fuel bills. For example:

> A trader sells a prop to a group for £100. This is a 'supply', which is subject to the standard rate of VAT. The group will therefore have to pay £100 plus VAT of £17.50. If the trader's raw materials to build the prop cost £10 plus £1.75 VAT, the output tax of £17.50 less the input tax of £1.75 is paid to Customs & Excise.

> A bookshop sells a script to a group for £10. This is also a 'supply', but one which is subject to a zero rate of VAT. The group therefore pays £10 for the script.

Thresholds and registration requirements: Where a group's standard-rated and zero-rated transactions in any twelve-month period exceed the annual registration limit, or there are reasonable grounds for expecting that the annual registration limit will be exceeded in the next thirty days, registration for VAT is compulsory. The registration threshold is £54,000 for 2001. There are penalties for late registration. For example:

> The prop-making trader has an annual turnover of standard-rated goods amounting to £55,000. The trader must register for VAT.

It is possible to register for VAT on a voluntary basis which may be favourable if the VAT payable on inputs is high, but VAT would then have to be charged on all standard-rated outputs made. This could result in an overall saving, but may be at the cost of substantial paperwork. If everything a group supplies is exempt or outside the scope of VAT, it will not be able to register for VAT and therefore cannot reclaim input tax.

Once registered for VAT, the group will need to show its VAT registration number on invoices and keep detailed records. Quarterly returns must be completed within one month of the end of that quarter, unless Customs & Excise agree to accept annual returns. Permission will normally be granted if the turnover of the group is less than £600,000 (from 2001).

The following examples of when VAT is payable will give some indication of the likely treatment of some of your group's activities. However, specialist tax advice should be sought.

Subscriptions: If members pay an annual subscription to a VAT-registered group, those subscriptions will be subject to VAT at the standard rate. If the member receives nothing back in return for the subscription, it may be possible to class the amount paid as a donation.

Donations: Gifts are outside the scope of VAT, which means that no VAT is chargeable. It may be necessary to ensure that a payment which is part subscription and part donation can be clearly separated into its two constituent parts. All documents should make it clear that any part which is a donation is freely given. If entrance to an event is part ticket price and part donation, the ticket price cannot be less than the usual price of the seats at a normal commercial event of the same type, otherwise Customs & Excise will treat both ticket price and donation as taxable.

Grants, insurance settlements and compensation payments are all outside the scope of VAT.

Ticket sales: Admission charges to cultural events organised by non-profit organisations which are managed and administered on a voluntary basis are exempt from VAT. For this purpose, performance of any form of stage play, opera, musical comedy, classical music, jazz, ballet or dance is accepted by the tax authorities as cultural. The non-profit organisation must invest any surplus in the improvement of the cultural facilities to which admission is provided. If the group makes any payment for managerial or administrative services it will not be eligible for exemption. However, reimbursement of expenses, audit charges, and honoraria will not necessarily prevent the exemption applying. If this exception does not apply, the income from ticket sales may still be exempt if the event can be classed as a fund-raising exercise.

Fund-raising events: Charitable and most not-for-profit organisations can also treat fund-raising events (such as a ball, dinner-dance, gala, show or performance, fête, exhibition, jumble sale, sponsored walk, quiz, etc.) as VAT-exempt. Note that social events which incidentally make a profit do not fall within this category. Also excluded from this category are normal trading activities (such as a charity shop). If part of an entrance fee represents a donation, that part will be outside the scope of VAT but the donation element must be freely given and must not be a condition of entry. A group must not hold more than fifteen fund-raising events of the same kind in any one location in any one year, or the exemption will be lost. The fifteen-event limit does not apply to fund-raising events where the gross takings from all similar events are no more than £1,000 per week. Therefore a coffee morning which raises £500 will not be included in the fifteen-event limit.

Sale or hire of goods: Unless part of a fund-raising event, these will be standard-rated, unless the goods in question are zero-rated. Zero-rated goods include printed material, such as programmes, commemorative brochures and books. Children's clothes, including commemorative T-shirts are zero-rated, but adult T-shirts will be standard-rated, unless sold at a fund-raising event, when the income will be exempt.

Sponsorship is standard-rated income for VAT purposes when it is received in return for a supply – for example advertising in a programme – unless it was received as part of a fund-raising event, in which case it will be exempt. Packages where nothing is received in return may be classed as a donation.

Publicity: Advertising space provided by a group on a noticeboard, a wall display, in a programme, magazine or on a poster is standard-rated, unless part of a fund-raising event, when it may be zero-rated. If a charity pays for advertising, it is zero-rated. Non-registered charities should inform the printer or other supplier to ensure that VAT is not charged.

Building projects: Most rental income from land and buildings will be exempt from VAT, but the landlord could opt to charge VAT. Also, if the group receives income which is exempt from VAT, restrictions can apply to the recovery of VAT on new theatre-building projects. These are complex areas and assistance should be obtained from a professional VAT specialist in these areas.

Recovery of VAT on expenditure: If a group is registered for VAT and receives only standard- and zero-rated income, it will be able to reclaim all of the VAT it is charged on its expenditure. However, if the group also receives exempt income it will only be able to recover all its input tax if the exempt input tax is less than the de minimis limit (£7,500 per annum in 2001). If the exempt input tax is more than the de minimis limit, then only some of the VAT charged on expenditure is recoverable.

A group organises a fund-raising barn dance, which raises £8,000. This income is exempt from VAT. It also received £72,000 from hiring and selling scenery, costumes and props. These are standard-rated. Because some of the group's income is standard-rated, and some is exempt from VAT, it can only recover a proportion of its output tax.

If in the following year, the same group received the same £72,000 from hiring and sales of scenery, etc., but only raises £7,000 from fund-raising, all of the output tax would be recoverable, because the amount of the income exempt from VAT is less than the de minimis limit.

Records and accounts: HM Customs & Excise require that records are maintained in sufficient detail to enable their officers to check the figures made on a VAT return. Records must be retained for a period of six years.

CORPORATION TAX

Corporation tax is charged on the profits and capital gains of companies and unincorporated associations. The amount of taxable profit is calculated by subtracting allowed deductions from taxable income. The amount of taxable capital gain is calculated on the increase in value of a capital asset between receipt and disposal (with an allowance for inflation). Rates of income tax vary, depending on the level of profits. The lowest rate of 10% applies for groups with profits under £10,000, rising to 30% for groups with profits over £1.5 million (2001).

> The prop-making trader makes a profit of £5,000 on trading income. If the trader has no allowed deductions, corporation tax of £500 is payable. If in the same year, the trader also sells a workshop for £30,000, which was bought for £27,000 (assuming a zero inflation rate for simplicity), tax will also be payable at the same 10% rate on the gain of £3,000.

A corporation tax year ends on 31 March. Liability to corporation tax involves paying any tax due nine months after the group's accounting-year end and making an annual corporation tax self-assessment return to the Inland Revenue within twelve months of its year end. Records must be retained for six years to allow for Inland Revenue scrutiny.

Non-taxable income: Some income, including donations and grants, is non–taxable. Therefore no tax is payable. As a concession, the Inland Revenue does not currently seek to tax profits made on fund-raising events if:

- the fund-raising event fulfils the conditions laid down for VAT exemption
- the profits are applied to charitable purposes

The Inland Revenue has published a booklet on fund-raising jointly with Customs & Excise which should help bring the two tax regimes closer together.

In any event, profits made on the sale of donated goods (at jumble sales or auctions, for example) are not taxed if the goods have not been significantly changed or refurbished.

Subscriptions or other contributions made by members to the group's funds will be treated like a donation, but fees charged for a particular service (like venue hire fee for a private party) will be taxable trading income.

Taxable income: Income from property, bank interest and trading is taxable. Where a group is offering general public entertainment and access to bar and catering facilities, so that its activities are broadly similar to a commercial theatre operation, it is more likely to be carrying out a taxable trade. The criteria for establishing whether a trade is being carried out are known as 'the badges of trade' and include an intention to make a profit. While the group's operation as a whole may be conducted on a non–profit basis, some activities (e.g. the bar) may be carried out with a view to profit with the intention of subsidising others (e.g. ticket prices).

Claiming expenses: If subscription fees are used to pay the day-to-day running expenses, then the expenses will not be taken into account in calculating corporation tax liability. If expenses are incurred in generating a trading profit, then these are normally allowed to be deducted from the taxable profit as an allowance.

A group's annual accounts show that it hired out its theatre venue to other organisations and received rent of £1,000. Members paid £250 in subscriptions and the group received £50 in gross bank interest on its deposit account. The group borrowed from a bank to buy its own venue and the accounts show that it paid £100 in interest. They also show that the group paid £500 in property repairs.

The group may offset its expenses (including loan interest) against its rental income, so that only the net profit is taxable. Corporation tax will therefore be payable on £1,000 plus £50 minus £100 minus £500 equals £450. The £250 subscriptions are not included in the calculation, since they are not taxable.

Reducing corporation tax liabilities: A group could separate its charitable work from its trading activities. Trading profits arising from the charity's primary purpose (such as selling theatre tickets) and incidental profits (for example from a bar and catering) could be exempt from income and corporation tax as long as the profits are applied solely for the purpose of the charity. Profits arising from non-primary purpose trading (such as hiring costumes or props to third parties) will be taxable, as will be the letting of theatre premises for functions. This tax charge can be avoided if:

- the profits are used for charitable purposes
- the trading activity is part only of the group's main function
- the group's turnover is less than £5,000 per year, or trading income is less than £50,000 and the trading income is less than 25% of the total income of the group (2001)

If the group's trading income does not fall within this limited exemption, another way of reducing the tax payable is to set up a trading subsidiary company which pays its annual profits to the charity. This enables the charity to recover the tax paid by the trading subsidiary.

Alternatively, establishing a group as a members' club may have tax advantages because surpluses arising from transactions with full members are regarded as 'mutual' and are thus not taxable. This means that club subscriptions and bar and catering surpluses from dealings with members (and their guests as long as the supply is made to the member) will be treated as not liable to corporation tax. Sales of tickets and profits from bar and catering services arising from transactions with non-members remain taxable.

Tax on a capital gain (for example, if the group sells its property at a profit) is not payable if the gain is used for charitable purposes.

PAYE

A group may make payments to creative team members or people helping with administration beyond pure reimbursement of their expenses. It is important in these circumstances to establish the nature of the relationship between the group and these individuals, particularly whether they are employed or self-employed. Differentiating between employed and self-employed staff is fraught with possible difficulties but at the extremes it is easy to recognise the difference between an employee and a self-employed contractor. For example, a full-time box-office staff member will normally be an employee, but the independent accountant who audits the theatre's accounts will not normally be an employee of the theatre. Broadly speaking, an employee will work where the employer requests, for an agreed number of hours per week, at an agreed rate of pay and will be subject to the control of the employer. Self-employed people on the other hand will be those who are running their own business, do not work exclusively for one person and will not be subject to the same level of control. They are likely to be at greater financial risk in conducting their business, having to meet any losses as well as taking the profits. The same criteria apply to casual, short-term, temporary or part-time workers, and the tests need to be applied separately to the circumstances of each engagement where an individual has more than one.

Where a group employs staff, it is responsible for operating the pay as you earn scheme (PAYE) and accounting for the employer's and the employee's National Insurance contributions (NIC). This means that the employer deducts the employee's income tax and National Insurance contributions from the employee's wages, and passes them directly to the Inland Revenue.

A group that employs a general manager will have to operate PAYE and account for NIC.

A group that pays a director to produce a show may be using a self-employed contractor, who will be responsible for his or her own income tax and NI payments.

The employer's PAYE obligations consist, in outline, of:

- deducting tax and employees' NIC from employees' wages or salaries weekly or monthly in accordance with the PAYE tax tables supplied by the Inland Revenue and maintaining tax deductions working sheets
- accounting to the Collector of Taxes monthly for the PAYE and employees' and employer's NIC. Employer's NIC is payable by the employer in addition to the employees' salary at the rate of up to 11.9% (2001) of the salary
- making end-of-year returns after 5 April annually, including details of any benefits in kind provided to employees

It may be tempting, in view of the additional cost and work involved, to categorise staff as self-employed rather than employees. If there is any doubt about whether an individual is self-employed, the safest course of action is to operate PAYE. Payments to self-employed individuals should only be made against proper invoices, as should payments to individuals operating through a personal service company, i.e. a company set up to provide their services. The group is at risk of being met with a charge for the tax and NIC which should have been paid and penalties and interest if it fails to operate PAYE properly.

Following successful litigation against the Inland Revenue the tax authorities now accept that actors and musicians engaged under standard Equity contracts should generally be treated as self-employed, so income tax (PAYE) does not apply to payments made to them. The majority of performers will, however, be treated as employees for National Insurance purposes and the group will be responsible for collecting employees' NIC and accounting for it and the associated employer's NIC to the Collector of Taxes. Directors and creative team members, such as designers, are likely to be self-employed unless working exclusively for one group.

Payments made to performers who are not resident in the UK are subject to a withholding tax administered by the Inland Revenue's Foreign Entertainers Unit, now part of the Special Compliance Office, Birmingham, which is extremely helpful in advising on withholding tax obligations.

BUSINESS RATES

Non-domestic property is subject to business rates, charged on an assumed annual rental value of the property. Places of religious worship belonging to the Church of England and the Church of Wales (or certified under statutory regulations) are exempt from business rates. Church halls and similar buildings under the same ownership are also exempt. Not-for-profit organisations (even though they are not charities) may qualify for relief from payment. A charity is entitled to an 80% rebate of business rates and the local authority may, at its discretion, waive the remaining 20%.

STAMP DUTY

This is a tax paid on sales of land, leases and transfers of shares and other securities. The rate for property transfers is calculated on a sliding scale which starts at zero for transfers of up to £60,000 going up to 4% for transfers over £500,000 (2001). Stamp duty is not payable if a charity buys or leases property (but the document must still be sent to the Stamp Duty Office so that they can record the exemption).

TAX RELIEF FOR DONORS AND THE GIFT AID SCHEME

Businesses get tax relief if they make charitable donations of cash, either for one-off or regular payments, with no lower or upper limits. They can also receive relief if they donate an item manufactured, supplied or used in the normal course of their trade.

Sponsorship payments qualify for tax relief if they are made in return for some publicity which represents a reasonable return on the outlay.

Under the now simplified Gift Aid Scheme, charities can recover from the Inland Revenue an amount equal to the basic-rate tax paid on the donation by an individual. This is currently equivalent to an extra 22% (2001). Since 2000, there has been no minimum amount for donations which qualify. The individual must pay at least as much tax as the charity will reclaim in the relevant year, not receive excessive benefits in return for the gift and make a declaration that the donations should be treated as Gift Aid donations. Longer term arrangements, often by way of deed of covenant, are also now covered by the Gift Aid Scheme.

If in a tax year an individual makes various donations to charities of £500, the charities may reclaim £141.03 (500 x 22/78), so that the donations will be worth £641.03. If the individual is a higher rate taxpayer, s/he can claim higher rate relief of £115.38 (641.03 x 18/100) on the gross donation. This means that for donations which cost the donor £384.62 (£500 − £115.38), the charities actually receive £641.03!

Inheritance tax at 40% is charged on the value of a deceased's estate if over £242,000 (2001). However, in addition to the exemption for transfers of the estate to a spouse, a further exemption exists for donations and bequests to charities.

Closure

If it is no longer feasible for a group to operate, perhaps because of falling numbers of members or supporters, it may be necessary to wind down the group's operations. If a group is keeping financial records, it should be able to identify if expenditure exceeds income, or if there are debts that it is unable to pay. Despite good planning, these situations sometimes arise, especially if funding sources change unexpectedly.

It is essential to address financial difficulties as soon as possible to prevent insolvency. As pointed out above, members of the governing body of an unincorporated association will almost certainly be responsible for the liabilities of the group. Members of the governing body of companies limited by guarantee may become personally responsible if they do not take every step to protect creditors. It is therefore important for a group facing these difficulties to obtain expert advice as soon as possible.

Once the issue has been identified, it may be possible to redress the position by reducing costs or increasing income. This may be possible by joining with another group to reduce overheads or by increasing subscription income.

If no rescue plan is possible, it will be necessary to wind up the group. For unincorporated associations, the rule book will normally set down the procedure to follow. Most will state that following a decision to wind up, final accounts should be prepared and all liabilities paid off. Any remaining assets are distributed to another similar organisation. If there are insufficient funds to pay all liabilities, this becomes an issue for the officers of the group. Ultimately, they may have to pay all debts from their personal resources, although it may be worth investigating the position with the creditors after discussing the situation with a solicitor.

For ADSL:

19 The Society may be dissolved by resolution at any General Meeting provided that the resolution is passed by a majority of at least 75% of the members present at the meeting. The Committee shall be responsible for the winding up of the Society, and any assets remaining after the discharge of the Society's debts shall be given to a charity nominated by the Committee.

For companies limited by guarantee, a decision to wind up may be made by the members or by a creditor. In the latter case, an accountant will be appointed to supervise the winding up of the group in accordance with the Insolvency Act 1986.

4 Reference section

Legal Glossary

acceptance   reaching agreement on the terms of an offer.

account of profits   a type of relief granted by the court, often in breach of copyright cases, which obliges the wrongdoer to pay to the innocent person all of the profits made from the breach.

accounts   a written summary of an organisation's financial situation.

action   a claim brought before a court.

act of God   something that happens due to natural causes which could not be reasonably foreseen.

Act of Parliament   a document which sets out legal rules passed by government.

annual general meeting (AGM)   companies must, and other organisations may, hold a members' meeting every year. This type of meeting normally considers the group's accounts (possibly including the auditor's report) and deals with elections. The governing document normally sets out how much notice is required for an AGM (normally at least twenty-one days).

annual return   companies must send a summary of its up-to-date information to Companies House on a form sent to the company's registered office every year.

arbitration   a formal mechanism for reaching agreement that parties in dispute can use as an alternative to litigation.

articles of association   part of the rule book for companies which may adopt a standard form set out in the Companies Act, 1985.

assignment   the transfer of the benefit of a contract from one person to another.

attestation   the signing (or execution) of a document.

auditor a qualified independent accountant who checks the organisation's financial records and certifies that they meet the required standard.

balance sheet the part of the group's financial records which records a summary of its assets and liabilities at a defined date.

bare licensee a person who has an informal, personal arrangement to use land or buildings which can be revoked at any time by the landlord.

barrister a qualified lawyer, and member of the Bar Council, who traditionally specialises in court appearances and other specialist work. Normally only used in conjunction with a solicitor.

beneficial owner the person who is entitled to the use of land or another asset for his or her own benefit.

board the governing body of directors or trustees.

books of account the financial records for the organisation, whether held on paper or computer.

breach of contract a failure of a party to an agreement to fulfil their obligations.

breach of trust a failure of a trustee or director to act properly, which may lead to personal liability for any loss caused to an organisation.

business name for companies, a name that is used which is different to the name registered at Companies House.

case law legal rules which are set out in decisions of the courts, often interpreting statute law.

certificate of incorporation the document issued by Companies House which sets out the company's name and registered number.

charity an organisation that has aims and objectives which are charitable.

Charity Commission an organisation which governs the administration of charities in England and Wales.

child a young person. Different laws set out different age ranges for children.

clause a section of an agreement.

club an organisation with rules that all members must obey. Clubs may operate as a business for profit.

common law legal rules based on decisions made by courts, rather than statutes.

Companies Register the database of companies (and related information about members and directors) kept at Companies House.

Companies Registry the organisation, also known as Companies House, which collates company information.

company an organisation with members created in accordance with the rules set down in statute.

company name the name of a company which is recorded at Companies House.

company secretary the officer of the company with administrative responsibilities. Compulsory for all companies.

consideration the price which passes between the parties to a contract. Consideration may be money, or something else of worth.

contract a binding agreement.

copyright the right to prevent anyone from copying an original work, as set out in statute.

covenant an obligation or promise.

damages compensation awarded by a court.

data protection rules relating to the use of personal information.

deed a formal written document which is legally binding.

director an officer of a company responsible for its day-to-day management.

disclaimer a declaration which limits liability.

discrimination unfair treatment.

engrossment the final copy of an agreement prepared for signature.

equity part of the law which originally developed as a more flexible alternative to common law, still particularly strong in trust law, or a share in a limited company.

eviction   the removal of a person from land or buildings.

execution   the formal process of entering into a legally binding written agreement.

extraordinary general meeting (EGM)   members' meetings which take place between annual general meetings. May also be called special general meetings.

extraordinary resolution   a decision made by a defined percentage of the members voting – usually 75%.

fiduciary   a special type of duty of utmost good faith owed by trustees to their trust, and directors to their company.

force majeure   a situation which is completely outside the control of a party – including natural disasters.

honorarium   a payment made to a person, even though that person rendered services without charge.

implied term   part of an agreement which was not agreed expressly by the parties, but included in the arrangement either by statute or the courts.

incorporation   the formation of a company.

injunction   a court order which prevents a person from a particular course of action.

intellectual property   the group of intangible rights, capable of ownership, which includes patents, trademarks, copyright and design rights.

joint and several   liability can be enforced either against a number of parties together, or against any one party separately.

lease   a contractual arrangement where an owner of land grants exclusive possession of that land to another person for an agreed period.

lessee   the tenant under a lease.

lessor   the person or body granting a lease.

licence   permission granted by one person to another.

licensee   a person to whom a licence is granted.

limited company   an incorporated body, whose members' responsibility is limited. The limit is set either by the amount of shares the member purchases, or the amount of the guarantee given.

mandate   permission granted by one person to another (for example, by members to a bank to honour cheques signed by two committee members).

memorandum of association   part of the rule book for companies which sets out the company's name, the whereabouts of its registered office, its principle purposes, amount of share capital (if any) and the fact that it is a limited liability company.

minutes   the written record of meetings.

negligence   a breach of duty caused by carelessness.

nuisance   something which interferes with the rights of another person.

offer   the first step of making a contract, which, if accepted for consideration, forms the terms of the agreement.

ordinary resolution   a decision made by a defined percentage of the members voting – usually 50%.

parties   persons or organisations who are named in a contract or other transaction or litigation.

passing off   misleading the public by adopting the look, feel or name belonging to someone else.

performers' rights   the rights of a performer in the live performance of their work, which prevents anyone else recording the work without permission.

profit and loss account   a part of an organisation's financial records, which summaries the amount of income and expenditure during a period.

quorum   the minimum number of people who must be present to allow a meeting to take place, often defined in the organisation's governing documents.

ratification   the approval of a past decision or action, taken without proper authority.

registered land   land which has had its ownership registered at HM Land Registry.

registered office   the address of a company which is recorded at Companies House.

registrar   an official in charge of a registration process.

rent   payment to a landlord or lessor in return for permission to use or occupy land.

restrictive covenant   a promise not to do something.

shadow director   a person who is not a director, but nevertheless performs the functions of a director, and therefore automatically assumes the obligations of that office.

solicitor   a lawyer who has fulfilled the entry criteria set down by the Law Society, and is regulated by that body, who provides advice on legal matters to clients.

statute   an Act of Parliament.

statutory instrument   regulations which are made by a government minister or other person or body with delegated responsibility in accordance with an Act of Parliament.

subsidiary company   a company which is owned by another body, rather than individual members.

tenant   the person who uses or occupies land owned by another person.

term   a provision in an agreement, or a period of time, especially in a lease.

tort   a wrongful act (or omission) which causes damage or injury to another person or property.

trademark   a distinctive logo or other symbol, words, shape or smell which distinguishes the goods or services of an organisation.

trust   a person holds property for the benefit of others.

trustee the person who holds the property on behalf of the beneficiaries.

ultra vires an act which goes beyond the powers granted to a person or organisation.

vicarious liability liability which is automatically assumed by someone for the wrongs committed by someone else – for example, an employer can be vicariously liable for the acts of its employees.

Further Reading

About Acting, Peter Barkworth, Methuen (2001)
Amateur Theatre Yearbook 2000, Jill Streatfeild, Platform Publications (1999)
Arts Organisations and Rights of Access etc, Mary Holland, Arts Council of England (1999)

Bums on Seats, Helen Sharman, A & C Black (1992)

Costume and Make-Up, Michael Holt, Phaidon Press (1988)
Create Your Own Stage Productions, Gill Davies, A & C Black (2000)

Data Protection for Voluntary Organisations, Paul Ticher, Directory of Social Change (2000)
Developing Your Organisation, Alan Lawrie, Directory of Social Change (2000)
Directing Amateur Theatre, Geoff Morris Mitchell, Northcote Publishers (1996)
Directing a Play, Michael McCaffery, Phaidon Press (1988)
Disability Discrimination Act 1995, Caroline Gooding, Arts Council of England (1999)

Electrical Safety at Places of Entertainment, HSE (1997)
Entertainment Licensing Law and Practice, Colin Manchester, Butterworth (1999)
Entertainments Licensing Law and Practice, Duncan Robinson, Roger Butterfield and David Chambers, Old Bailey Press (1999)

Essential Guide to Business in the Performing Arts, Vivien Freakley and Rachel Sutton, Hodder & Stoughton (1996)

Essential Guide to Stage Management Lighting & Sound, Scott Palmer, Hodder & Stoughton (2000)

Essessial Theatre, Crispin Raymond, Arts Council of England (1999)

The Event Safety Guide, HSE (1999)

Fight, Direction for Stage and Screen, William Hobbs, A & C Black (1995)

The Fundraisers Guide to the Law, Bates Wells and Braithwaite, Centre for Voluntary Sector Development, Directory of Social Change (2000)

The Health & Safety Handbook for Voluntary & Community Organisations, Al Hinde and Charlie Kavanagh, Director of Social Change (1998)

Hi concept – lo tech: Theatre for everyone in any place, Barbara Carlisle and Don Drapeau, Heinemann (1996)

How to Be Fringe Safe, The Festival Fringe Society (1999)

How to Do a Show on the Fringe, The Festival Fringe Society (1999)

Impro, Keith Johnstone, Methuen (1981)

In on the Act, Eve Blizzard, Pipers' Ash (1999)

Just About Managing?, Sandy Adirondack, London Voluntary Service Council (1998)

Latex and You, HSE Books (2000)

The Legal Guide for Involving Young People as Volunteers, Clair Byran and Esther Thompson, Islington Volunteer Centre (2000)

Lighting and Sound, Neil Fraser, Phaidon Press (1988)

A Management Companion for Voluntary Organisations, Tim Cook and Guy Braithwaite, Directory of Social Change (2000)

Managing Conflict, Gill Taylor, Directory of Social Change (1999)

Model Rules of Management for Places of Public Entertainment, Association of British Theatre Technicians (1998)

A Modern Approach to Emergency Lighting in Theatres, Association of British Theatre Technicians (1995)

Musicals: The Guide to Amateur Production, Peter Spencer, J. Garnet Miller (1993)

A Practical Guide to Accounting by Charities, Kate Sayer, Directory of Social Change (1996)

Running a Charity, Francesca Quint, Jordans (1994)

Safe to Grow, Anne Dunkley, Baptist Union (1998)

Smoke and Vapour Effects Used in Entertainment, HSE (1998)

Stage Design and Properties, Michael Holt, Phaidon Press (1992)

Stage Management and Theatre Administration, Pauline Menear and Terry Hawkins, Phaidon Press (1988)

Stage Management: The Essential Handbook, Gail Pallin, Queensgate Publications (2000)

Stages for Tomorrow, Francis Reid, Focal Press (1998)

The Staging Handbook, Francis Reid, A & C Black (2001)

Technical Standards for Places of Entertainment, ABTT (2001)

Theatre Games, Clive Barker, Methuen (1977)

Voluntary but not Amateur, Jacki Reason, Ruth Hayes and Duncan Forbes, London Voluntary Service Council (2000)

The Voluntary Sector Legal Handbook, Sandy Adirondack and James Sinclair Taylor, Directory of Social Change (2001)

Working at Heights in the Broadcasting & Entertainment Industries, HSE (1998)

Working with Animals in Entertainment, HSE Books (1996)

Useful Addresses

Adapt Trust
8 Hampton Terrace, Edinburgh EH12 5JD
tel 0131 346 1999 *fax* 0131 346 1991
web www.adapttrust.co.uk

Advice on access for disabled people to arts premises.

Advertising Standards Authority
2 Torrington Place, London WC1E 7HW
tel 020 7580 5555 *fax* 020 7631 3051
web www.asa.org.uk

Provider of advice relating to advertising.

Amateur Stage
Hampden House, 2 Weymouth Street, London W1N 3FD
tel 020 7636 4343 *fax* 020 7636 2323
web www.amdram.co.uk/amstage1.htm

Publisher of monthly magazine.

Amdram
PO Box 536, Norwich MLO NR6 7JZ
tel 07050 803635
web www.amdram.co.uk

Comprehensive web site.

Animal Consultants and Trainers Association (ACTA)
Warwick House, 181-3 Warwick Road, London W14 8PU
tel 020 7244 6900 *fax* 020 7370 2823
web www.acta4animals.com

Association for animal trainers.

Arts Council of England
14 Great Peter Street, London SW1P 3NQ
tel 020 7333 0100 *fax* 020 7973 6590
web www.artscouncil.org.uk

Responsible for the development and funding of the arts in England.

Arts Council of Wales
Holst House, 9 Museum Place, Cardiff CF1 3NX
tel 029 2037 6500 *fax* 029 2022 1447
web www.ccc-acw.org.uk

Responsible for the development and funding of the arts in Wales.

Association of British Theatre Technicians (ABTT)
47 Bermondsey Street, London SE1 3XT
tel 020 7403 3778 *fax* 020 7378 6170
web www.abtt.org.uk

Provides information and training on theatre planning and stage management.

Association of Lighting Designers (ALD)
PO Box 89, Welwyn Garden City AL7 1ZW
tel 01707 891 848 *fax* 01707 891 848
web: www.ald.org.uk

Professional body representing lighting designers.

British Federation of Festivals for Music, Dance and Speech
Festivals House, 198 Park Lane, Macclesfield SK11 6UD

tel 01625 428297 *fax* 01625 503229
web www.festivals.demon.co.uk

Umbrella organisation for festivals.

Central Council for Amateur Theatre
c/o 29 Glenhurst Court, Farquhar Road, London, SE19 1SR
tel 020 8761 1273

Umbrella organisation for national amateur theatre organisations.

Charity Commission for England and Wales
Harmsworth House, 13-15 Bouverie Street, London EC4Y 8DP
tel 0870 333 0123 *fax* 020 7674 2300
web www.charity-commission.gov.uk

Guidance on registration and management of charities.

Commission for Racial Equality
Elliot House, 10-12 Allington Street, London SW1E 5EH
tel 020 7828 7022 *fax* 020 7630 7605
web www.cre.gov.uk

Advice relating to race relations.

Committee of Advertising Practice (CAP)
tel 020 7580 4100 *fax* 020 7580 4072
web www.cap.org.uk

Provides advice on whether advertising meets the Advertising Code of Practice.

Community Matters
12-20 Baron Street, London W1 9LL
tel 020 7226 0189 *fax* 020 7354 9570
web www.communitymatters.org.uk

Publications and training for groups who support needs of their communities.

Companies House
Crown Way, Cardiff CF4 3UZ
tel 0870 333 3636 *fax* 029 2038 0900
web www.companies-house.gov.uk

Registration and management of incorporated associations (companies and limited partnerships) in England and Wales.

Contemporary Music Making for Amateurs (COMA)
Toynbee Studios, 28 Commercial Street, London E1 6LS
tel 020 7247 7736 *fax* 020 7247 7732
web www.coma.org

Network for people creating music for amateurs.

Customs & Excise
see telephone directory for local office
web www.hmce.gov.uk

Value Added Tax information.

Data Protection Commissioner
see *Office of the Information Commissioner*

Directors Guild of Great Britain
314–320 Gray's Inn Road, London WC1X 8DP
tel 020 7278 4343 *fax* 020 7278 4742
web www.dggb.co.uk

Members organisation for directors.

Directory of Social Change
24 Stephenson Way, London NW1 2DP
tel 020 7209 5151
web www.dsc.org.uk

Publications and training on large range of social and community-related topics.

Disability Rights Commission
Freepost MID 02164, Stratford-upon-Avon CV37 9BR
tel 08457 622 633 *fax* 08457 778 878
web www.drc-gb.org

Advice relating to disability discrimination.

Drama Association of Wales
The Old Library, Singleton Road, Splott, Cardiff CF24 2ET
tel 029 2045 2200 *fax* 029 2045 2277
web www.amdram.co.uk/drama-association-wales

Umbrella organisation for Welsh amateur and youth theatre, and
guardian for the former British Theatre Association playscripts
lending collection.

Equal Opportunities Commission
Arndale House, Arndale Centre, Manchester M4 3EQ
tel 0161 833 9244 *fax* 0161 838 8312
web www.eoc.org.uk

Advice in relation to sex discrimination.

Equality Direct
tel 0845 600 3444
web www.equalitydirect.org.uk

Government body which provides advice on discrimination matters.

Equity
Guild House, Upper St Martin's Lane, London WC2H 9EG
tel 020 7379 6000 *fax* 020 7379 7001
web www.equity.org.uk

Members organisation for professional actors.

Guild of Drama Adjudicators
c/o 14 Elmwood, Welwyn, Garden City AL8 6LE
tel 01707 326 488 *fax* 01707 326 488
web www.amdram.co.uk/goda/welcome.htm

Members organisation for adjudicators.

Health and Safety Executive (HSE)
Caerphilly Business Park, Caerphilly CF83 3GG
tel 0870 1545500
web www.hse.gov.uk

Practical advice and guides on all matters relating to health and safety.

Health and Safety Executive Mail Order
PO Box 1999, Sudbury CO10 6FS
tel 01787 881165 *fax* (for orders) 01787 313 995
web www.hsebooks.co.uk

Nick Hern Books Ltd
The Glasshouse, 49a Goldhawk Road, London W12 8QP
tel 020 8749 4953 *fax* 020 8746 2006

Publisher and agent.

Independent Theatre Council (ITC)
12 The Leather Market, Weston Street, London SE1 3ER
tel 020 7403 1727 *fax* 020 7403 1745
web www.itc-arts.org

Provides arts organisations with advocacy, legal and management advice, information and training services.

Inland Revenue
see telephone book for local office
web www.inlandrevenue.gov.uk

Tax and related subjects including Gift Aid Scheme.

Institute of Chartered Accountants in England and Wales
Chartered Accountants Hall, PO Box 433, London EC2P 2BJ
tel 020 7920 8100 *fax* 020 7920 0547
web www.icaew.co.uk

Professional body for accountants.

Institute of Chartered Accountants of Scotland
CA House, 21 Haymarket Yards, Edinburgh EH12 5BH
tel 0131 347 0100 *fax* 0131 347 0105
web www.icas.org.uk

Professional body for accountants.

International Dance Teachers' Association
International House, 76 Bennett Road, Brighton BN2 5JL
tel 01273 685 652 *fax* 01273 674 388
web www.idta.co.uk

Advisory body on all theatre-related dance.

Law Society of England and Wales
113 Chancery Lane, London WC2A 1PL
tel 020 7242 1222 *fax* 020 7831 0344
web www.lawsoc.org.uk

Professional body for solicitors.

Law Society of Scotland
26 Drumsheugh Gardens, Edinburgh EH3 7YR
tel 0131 226 7411 *fax* 0131 225 2934
web www.lawscot.org.uk

Professional body for solicitors.

Little Theatre Guild of Great Britain
c/o 181 Brampton Road, Carlisle CA3 9AX
tel 01228 522 649 *fax* 01228 522 649

web www.uktw.co.uk/clubs/ltg.htm

Members organisation for groups which control or own their own venue.

Mechanical Copyright Protection Society Limited
Elgar House, 41 Streatham High Road, London SW16 1ER
tel 020 8664 4400 *fax* 020 8378 7300
web www.mcps.co.uk

Represents composers, etc. and negotiates licences for recordings.

Musicians' Union
60 Clapham Road, London SW9 0JJ
tel 020 7582 5566 *fax* 020 7582 9805
web www.musiciansunion.org.uk

Member organisation for professional musicians.

MusicScope
95 White Lion Street, London N1 9PF
tel 020 7278 1133 *fax* 020 7278 4442

Publisher and agent.

National Association of Youth Theatres
Arts Centre, Vane Terrace, Darlington, DL3 7AX
tel 01325 363 330 *fax* 01325 363 313
web www.nayt.org.uk

Umbrella organisation for youth theatre groups.

National Council for Voluntary Organisations (NCVO)
Regent's Wharf, 8 All Saints Street, London N1 9RL
tel 020 7713 6161 *fax* 020 7713 6300
web www.ncvo-vol.org.uk

Publications, training and telephone advice.

National Disability Arts Forum
Mea House, Ellison Place, Newcastle-upon-Tyne NE1 8XS
tel 0191 261 1628 *fax* 0191 222 0573
web www.ndaf.org

Promoter of disability arts.

National Drama Festivals Association
c/o Bramleys, Main Street, Shudy Camps, Cambridge, CB1 6RA
tel 01799 584920 *fax* 01799 584921
web www.amdram.co.uk/ndfa

Umbrella organisation for festivals.

National Operatic & Dramatic Association (NODA)
NODA House, 1 Crestfield Street, London WC1H 8AU
tel 020 7837 5655 *fax* 020 7833 0609
Web www.noda.org.uk

Umbrella organisation for amateur drama groups.

NODA Insurance
1 High Street, Taunton TA1 3PG
tel 0870 241 1086 *fax* 01823 270357

Insurance provider.

Office of the Information Commissioner
Wycliffe House, Water Lane, Wilmslow SK9 5AF
tel 01625 545 745 *fax* 01625 524 510
web www.dataprotection.gov.uk

Advice for data protection regulations.

Open Performance Centre Limited
Unit 2, 67 Earl St, Sheffield S1 4PY
tel 0114 249 3650 *fax* 0114 249 3651
web www.opcentre.f9.co.uk
Workshops, courses and community projects.

Open Theatre Company Limited
Hilltop House, Hilltop Lane, Ombersley, Worcs WR9 0ES
tel 01905 620 631
web www.opentheatre.co.uk

Promotes training, research and development for community plays and learning disability.

Performing Right Society Foundation
29–33 Berners Street, London W1T 3AB
tel 020 7306 4044 *fax* 020 7306 4350
web www.prsf.co.uk

Grant-making body for new music.

Performing Rights Society
29–33 Berners Street, London W1T 3AB
tel 020 7580 5544
web www.prs.co.uk

Copyright licences.

Phonographic Performance Limited
1 Upper James Street, London W1R 3HG
tel 020 7534 1000 *fax* 020 7534 1111
web www.ppluk.com

Grants licences for public performance of sound recordings.

Professional Lighting and Sound Association (PLASA)
38 St Leonards Road, Eastbourne BN21 3UT
tel 01323 410 335 *fax* 01323 646 905
web www.plasa.org

Trade association for entertainment technology industry.

Really Useful Group Limited
22 Tower Street, London WC2H 9TW
tel 020 7240 0880 *fax* 020 7240 1204
web www.reallyuseful.com

Publisher, agent and production company.

Religious Drama Society of Great Britain (RADIUS)
1a Kennington Road, London SE1 7QP
tel 020 7401 2422

Provides advice on use and exploration of Christian drama.

RIDDOR Incident Contact Centre
Caerphilly Business Park, Caerphilly CF83 3GG
tel 0845 300 9923 *fax* 0845 300 9924
web www.riddor.gov.uk

Health and safety reporting authority.

Royal Society for Prevention of Cruelty to Animals (RSPCA)
Wilberforce Way, Southwater, Horsham, West Sussex RH13 7WN
tel 0870 333 5999 *fax* 0870 7530048
web www.rspca.org.uk

Charity promoting good practice for animals.

Samuel French Limited
52 Fitzroy Street, London W1T 5JR
tel 020 7387 9373 *fax* 020 7387 2161
web www.samuelfrench-london.co.uk

Bookshop, publisher and agent.

Scottish Arts Council

12 Manor Place, Edinburgh EH3 7DD
tel 0131 226 6051 *fax* 0131 225 9833
web www.sac.org.uk

Responsible for the development and funding of the arts in Scotland.

Scottish Community Drama Association

5 York Place, Edinburgh EH1 3EB
tel 0131 557 5552 *fax* 0131 557 5552
web www.scda.org.uk

Umbrella organisation for amateur theatre in Scotland.

Society of British Theatre Designers (SBTD)

47 Bermondsey Street, London SE1 3XT
tel 020 7403 3778 *fax* 020 7378 6170
web www.theatredesign.co.uk

Publishes guides and holds register of designers.

Stage Management Association

47 Bermondsey Street, London SE1 3XT
tel 020 7403 6655 *fax* 020 7378 6170
web www.stagemanagementassociation.co.uk

Supports and represents professional stage managers.

The Stage Newspaper Limited

Stage House, 47 Bermondsey Street, London SE1 3XT
tel 020 7403 1818 *fax* 020 7357 9287
web www.thestage.co.uk

The longest established entertainment trade weekly.

Voluntary Arts Network
PO Box 200, Cardiff CF5 1YH
tel 029 20 395 395 *fax* 029 20 397 397
web www.voluntaryarts.org

Produces publications, training and support throughout the UK.

Josef Weinberger Limited
12–14 Mortimer Street, London W1T 3JJ
tel 020 7580 2827 *fax* 020 7436 9616
web www.josef-weinberger.co.uk

Playscript publisher and agent.

Writers' Guild of Great Britain
430 Edgware Road, London W2 1EH
tel 020 7723 8074 *fax* 020 7706 2413
web www.writers.org.uk/guild

Writers' union.

Index of Statutes and Regulations

General Index